TAILORED LOOSE COVERS

TAILORED
LOOSE COVERS

Mary Davies

STANLEY PAUL
London Melbourne Sydney Auckland Johannesburg

Stanley Paul & Co. Ltd

An imprint of the Hutchinson Publishing Group

17–21 Conway Street, London W1P 6JD

Hutchinson Group (Australia) Pty Ltd
30–32 Cremorne Street, Richmond South, Victoria 3121
PO Box 151, Broadway, New South Wales 2007

Hutchinson Group (NZ) Ltd
32–34 View Road, PO Box 40-086, Glenfield, Auckland 10

Hutchinson Group (SA) Pty Ltd
PO Box 337, Bergvlei 2012, South Africa

First published 1982
© Mary Davies 1982

Set in VIP Baskerville by
A-Line Services, Saffron Walden, Essex

Printed in Great Britain by The Anchor Press Ltd
and bound by Wm Brendon & Son Ltd,
both of Tiptree, Essex

British Library Cataloguing in Publication Data
Davies, Mary
    Tailored loose covers.
    1. Slip covers
    I. Title
    646.2'13   TT395

ISBN 0 09 145661 4

CONTENTS

INTRODUCTION

It is ironic that in the bad old days of cheap labour loose covers were considered little better than dust sheets, to be whipped off when company arrived. Now that they are soft furnishings in their own right making charges for tailored covers are as much as, if not more than, the cost of the basic material.

Tastes have changed too. In the days of dust covers people bought furnishings to last a lifetime, then spent their lives protecting them. Nowadays people want loose covers as much for variety as to hide a well-worn suite. Well-made loose covers not only look far better than bought stretch covers. They can often give shabby but basically sound furniture a new lease of life and can be made to suit your own decor and taste in a way that even the very best new suite might not.

Perhaps more than anything it is the enormous improvement in the quality and design of materials that has been the 'making' of loose covers. With the advent of shrinkproofing and fadeproofing, and award-winning designs, covers made of a top quality material will not only last but will look good right to the end.

Tailored loose covers having become something of a luxury, the obvious recourse for anyone with a sewing machine and a general interest in sewing is to 'do-it-yourself', and you would expect to find a wealth of information on this worthwhile and rewarding craft.

Surprisingly there is not. The subject cannot easily be taught at an adult education centre because there are no paper patterns for covers and besides, you cannot tuck your chair under your arm and take it to class. The general practice with books on soft furnishings is to telescope the whole craft into one chapter. This hardly inspires confidence to invest a fair amount of money on costly material. Worse, it does a great injustice to the craft since it makes it appear more difficult than it is. Such sparse directions, of necessity limited to one or two types of chair, are hard to adapt for the many other styles that people would like to cover. It would of course be boring and repetitive to give set after set of instructions, each modified to some extent for a particular style of chair. I hope this book solves the problem in much the same way as the Identikit system builds up a picture of a wanted person. You simply choose from the many types of backs, arms, wings, etc., shown in the main sections, to build up a set of directions for your own particular chair – a system which, with a little ingenuity, can be adapted even for the most unusual styles.

In this respect there is a section on such unusual features as the roll back of a chesterfield, removable arms and so on. These directions have to be combined with those in the main sections, however, and I advise you to try something straightforward first to get the general idea of cover-making.

There is also a section on small covers, deliberately left to the last because small does not necessarily mean easy, and I hope that you will read the introduction to each stage before attempting small covers.

After gaining some experience on your own covers and perhaps those of friends, you may be interested in pursuing cover making as a trade, either in the workroom of a big store or at home as a part-time outworker.

Such outwork is better paid than most, and particularly useful for housebound women. You must be prepared to spend money on an industrial machine, but these are not hard to buy second hand and they soon pay for themselves.

When you have acquired sufficient professional experience you may wish to become a freelance outworker (as I did) with your own workroom and staff. Such freelancers offer their services to the many small shops that sell soft furnishing material but which do not have their own workrooms, and to the big stores which often have more work than they can handle. By now your skills should include the making of unlined and lined curtains, frills, pelmets, etc., for which you will require a large table.

Usually the shops and stores are content with the profit on the extra sales of materials that your services bring them, but some also expect to make a profit on making charges. Provided you are willing to make good any material you spoil, you should resist this, and never agree to accept responsibility for collecting the making charges. Once a cover is accepted by the customer the shop or store should pay you the prearranged fee.

Although a freelance earns much more than a tied outworker you should not launch out on your own until you have the experience and equipment, and initially you should not rely solely on cover making for an income. Demand is seasonal. You will have more work than you can cope with in the months before Christmas and in the spring. In between there will be lean times.

MARY DAVIES, 1982

ABBREVIATIONS

I/B – inside back	O/A – outside arm	F/A – front arm
O/B – outside back	I/W – inside wing	T/A – top arm
I/A – inside arm	O/W – outside wing	S&F – seat and front

1
QUESTIONS AND ANSWERS

There are several questions you will wish to ask before actually committing yourself. Most of the answers will reassure you and one or two may well save disappointment in one way or another. The most important question is:

CAN I DO IT?

If you can make a dress that you *would* be seen dead in, then you should be able to make a loose cover. But do not try to 'dress-make' a cover. Cover making is not difficult but it is *different*. It is a craft in its own right with its own rules and limitations.

A loose cover is not cut from a pattern like a dress. Chairs come in too many shapes and sizes for patterns to be practical. But in any case, cover making is more straightforward than that. You have an enormous advantage over dressmakers: your models are good-natured enough to stay put for hours on end and let you stick pins in them. You fit the material directly onto the chair.

WILL IT BE WORTH IT?

Yes. When covers are first put on a worn and faded three-piece suite it is most satisfying to see how the whole room is transformed. This can lead to covers becoming established as part of the decor: a cosy set for winter and a bright one for summer, perhaps to be changed with the curtains. Also worth the effort are covers to protect new furniture, especially when there are children about, and they can easily be removed for special occasions. (The covers as well as the children!)

WHAT CAN I COVER?

Almost anything, though a few chairs are impossible to cover and some are just not worth the trouble. Before you waste time and money on a job that will never be completely satisfactory, check here:

Leather or PVC upholstery

Loose covers will slip about and look untidy on leather or PVC no matter how well they are made. Such furniture is also very difficult to fit because the material moves out of position as you work.

Velvet, plush and corduroy upholstery

Do not cover for protection as the cover will rub patches in the pile or nap. Of course if the furniture is already threadbare then further wear will not matter. Loose covers also tend to ride a little on pile and will look bumpy.

Cane, wicker and wooden decoration

Cane and wicker will catch on the material, pull threads and wear holes where the cover comes into contact with rough edges. Wooden decorations will also wear holes eventually: so chairs with fixed upholstery surrounded by a wooden frame should not be covered.

Cottage furniture with box cushion-type backs and seats resting on wooden frames do not come into this category, and can be covered quite easily as can fireside chairs with wooden arms.

If the arms of fireside chairs are upholstered but have wooden tops, they can be covered over so long as the arms of the cover are lined with foam at the top. This not only protects the cover but provides something soft to lean on.

Buttoning, fluting, ridging and ruching

Furniture with these features can be covered, but you should appreciate before deciding on loose covers that the features which probably attracted you to the furniture in the first place will be concealed under the cover.

There is no satisfactory way of reproducing these upholstered effects in a loose cover. Figure 1 will give you an idea of the aftereffect of loose covers.

Figure 1

Inside backs

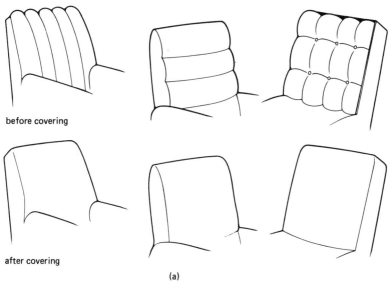

before covering

after covering

(a)

Head rolls   before and after covering

(b)

Front arms   before and after covering

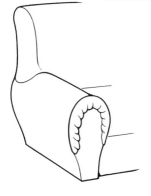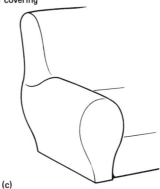

(c)

Overhanging arms

Fixed arms that overhang on the outside are difficult to work since the cover will sag underneath the arms (Figure 2a and b).

When the arms overhang a lot the problem can be overcome to some extent by hiding the difficult parts under a frill, although a frill looks somewhat out of place on such modern furniture. In this example the shape of the arms can be simplified and the parts at the sides of the overhang filled in from trimmings (Figure 2c).

If the overhang is slight it can be covered by extending the outside arm to cover most of the overhang and filling in the remainder from trimmings, as shown in Figure 2d. This would change the line of the chair slightly, but it would scarcely show.

Many overhanging arms are removable, however, and these can be fitted quite easily with their own small covers, as shown in Chapter 7.

Figure 2

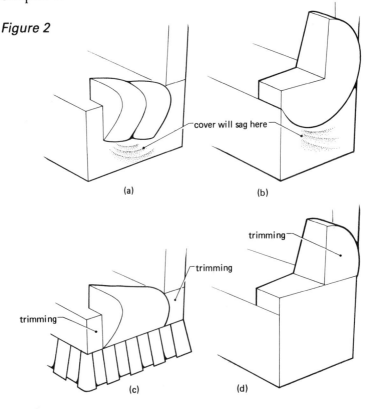

Cushion-type backs with upholstered frames

When the inside back of the chair is a separate cushion resting on an upholstered frame as in Figure 3a, cover the chair and the cushion-type back separately, and treat the latter as a stand-up boxed cushion.

Figure 3

(a)

(b)

A cushion-type back that is a fixture as in Figure 3b is not suitable for covering. The fitting of this back is very difficult, and the appearance of the finished cover hardly ever justifies the trouble taken.

Tub chair

Beginners sometimes make their first attempts on a tub chair because it is small and looks easy.

In fact the concave back is hard to fit because a straight piece of material will not lie flat against a curved surface without a great deal of manipulation. Also, the rounded seat requires a special collar for tucking into the recess around the seat.

This is another instance where the appearance of the cover will not be likely to justify the trouble taken to make it.

WHAT EQUIPMENT SHALL I NEED?

An electric or treadle sewing machine with a piping/zipper foot
Heavy machine needles
A large pair of scissors
Tape measure, preferably with a metal piece at one end
Dressmaking pins
Tailor's chalk
A 6 in (15 cm) rule is useful when making frilled covers

WHAT MATERIAL SHALL I BUY?

Material 48 in (122 cm) wide is generally best for loose covers, although 30–31 in (76–79 cm) material can, on rare occasions, be more economical. The directions in this book apply to material that is 48 in (122 cm) *between the selvedges*. Buy from a reputable soft furnishings dealer and make sure that it is cover material, not curtaining. Curtain material often looks suitable for covers but it is not strong enough. An experienced shop assistant will know the difference.

Suitable materials

Linen and linen union (a union of flax and cotton), chintz, soft repp, cretonne, brocade, damask and woollen or synthetic weave are all appropriate.

Washing or dry-cleaning

Whether you will want to wash or dry-clean the cover will of course depend to some extent on how quickly you expect it to get dirty. Frequent dry-cleaning to keep up with the accidents of a young family will prove expensive, but it can be risky to wash some materials. Also take into account that some covers may be too large for a washing machine or spin drier, and extra laundering facilities may be required.

Cottons and linens are washable, but to varying extents according to their quality. Some of the cheaper ones shrink so much they should be dry-cleaned. Woollen weaves should always be dry-cleaned.

Shrinkproof generally means that the material shrinks less than those not guaranteed, but shrinks nevertheless. For this reason some allowance is made for shrinkage in the following directions, although this is limited because the shape of the cover must not be spoilt – a baggy cover is ugly and cannot be tolerated when the object is to *tailor* a perfect fit.

However, surprisingly, most of what is lost in average shrinkage can be regained. Do not tumble dry. Press the cover while it is fairly damp, paying particular attention to a frill but only running the iron lightly over the body. Put the cover on the chair while it is still warm and damp, and gently stretch it back into shape. Finally, iron the cover on the chair.

UNSUITABLE MATERIALS

As stated previously, dressmaking and curtain materials are not strong enough for covers. The following are also unsuitable.

Any thick, heavy material, but especially upholsteries such as moquette
Machine needles will break by the score as you plough through seams four layers thick (the two pieces being sewn together plus the casing of the piping); and – where one seam crosses another – eight layers. A material does not have to be heavy and coarse to be durable.

Any loosely woven material
Loose weaves will pull out of shape not only as you fit and sew but afterwards, when the cover is on the chair. Pins fall out before you have time to trim the seams, and allowances fray away even with the gentlest handling. Loose weaves also do a poor job of keeping a chair clean because dust sinks right through them.

Folkweave and barkweave are in this category, being thick lengthwise strands loosely held together by cross-threads of black cotton.

Cheap repp
Repp is a plain material with small horizontal ridges. Good quality repps are quite suitable but the cheap kind is as stiff and unyielding as cardboard. Your fingers will be red-raw from forcing pins into it, and you will be unable to ease it over the rounded parts of the chair; consequently, the cover will stand away from the chair and look baggy.

Stretch bri-nylon
This is used for ready-made covers, the cover being made slightly too small for the chair so that its elasticity will give the illusion of a good fit. The drawback is that there are bound to be places where there is too much strain on the stretch, and the covers do not last long. The same will apply to your cover if you rely on elasticity for a fit – and then it would not be a *tailored* loose cover.

Stretch material is difficult to work with because it pulls out of shape when being fitted and when being sewn up.

PATTERNED OR PLAIN COVERS?

Patterned material

A large pattern in a small room is overpowering. Also do not use a large pattern on a small chair. If the extent of the pattern cannot be seen, or at least its main motif, it will have no form or balance.

Patterned materials are harder to cut and fit than plain ones because the main motif has to be centred on inside and outside backs, inside and outside arms, cushions, etc. When more than one item is being covered the same motif must show in the same place on each chair and settee.

Figure 4

(a) *wide inside back, middle motif centred*

(b) *top and bottom of boxed cushion, side motifs centred — and matching the inside back*

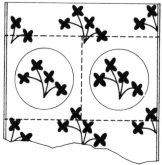

Extra material is required for matching because every time you cut you have to start at a place that will bring the main motif to the centre of the piece, and this nearly always means cutting out strips. On large covers the extra yardage involved in matching is not excessive because the strips can be used for other parts of the cover. When centring and matching the pattern on several small items, however, there can be a great deal of wastage. Avoid this by using an overall pattern rather than one with a distinct motif.

Suitable patterns. The best design for covers is a staggered pattern with all motifs the same (Figure 4) because the same motif

Figure 5

(a) *wide inside back, no alternative but to centre the middle motif*

(b) *top and bottom of boxed cushion, middle motif centred to match the inside back*

can be centred whether a full width is required or a half width. This means that if the inside back of your chair requires a full width, but the boxed cushion requires half widths only for the top and bottom, you can centre the middle motif for the back (Figure 4a) and those at the side for the top and bottom of the boxed cushion (Figure 4b) – and all the pieces will match.

Problems arise when a design has a main motif at the sides and a smaller, secondary motif in the middle (Figure 5). For a full-width back you have no alternative but to show the inferior motif (Figure 5a), which is unsatisfactory in itself; and if you cut half widths for the top and bottom of the boxed cushion, as in Figure 4b, they will not match the back. Since this is even more unsatisfactory, your only recourse is to show the inferior motif on the cushion also, which means using twice the amount actually needed for the cushion (Figure 5b).

Note, however, that if all the main pieces of a chair can be covered out of half widths, the pattern shown in Figure 5 will be quite suitable.

Figure 6

Two patterns side by side (Figure 6) cannot be used for pieces requiring full widths since neither motif will be seen in its entirety.

Suitable pattern repeats.   When using a pattern with a distinct motif for several small covers, centring and matching can prove wasteful unless you find suitable repeats. You can also work out a more accurate estimate for large covers by finding suitable repeats for the longest pieces.

The best repeat is one that gives a multiple near to, but not less than, the required length. For a length of 27 in (69 cm) for instance, 9 in (23 cm) would be perfect because three repeats work out to that amount exactly. Also good is 14 in (36 cm) because two repeats come to only 1 in (2.5 cm) more than the required length.

To estimate, add 9 in (23 cm) to the length of the first width for centring the pattern (since it is unlikely that the length of the material will start at a suitable place for this), and estimate the multiple of the chosen repeat for each remaining width.

Take as an example six dining chair seats for which you require pieces 22 in wide × 27 in (56 × 69 cm) long. The estimate in plain material would be three widths (two covers per width) × 27 in (69 cm) = 81 in (206 cm). In a patterned material the first two of the following estimates would be based on good repeats, while the third would be wasteful and the last disastrous:

Repeat	Nearest Multiple	Estimate:	Total
9″	3 × 9 ″ = 27″	1st width 36″ plus 2 widths × 27″ =	90″ (229 cm)
14″	2 × 14″ = 28″	1st width 36″ plus 2 widths × 28″ =	92″ (234 cm)
13″	3 × 13″ = 39″	1st width 36″ plus 2 widths × 39″ =	114″ (264 cm)
26″	2 × 26″ = 52″	1st width 36″ plus 2 widths × 52″ =	140″ (356 cm)

Finishing patterned covers. Traditionally, chintzy covers are finished with a gathered frill, more elegant patterns with a box-pleated frill. Also suitable is a skirt with inverted pleats at the corners, or a plain skirt in four parts. The traditional patterned cover does not look properly finished if plain-tailored, that is without a frill or skirt.

Ideas for patterned covers. Although embellishments are not generally needed, there are ways of ringing the changes. One is to cover the piping cord in a plain material that picks out the main colour of the pattern; another is to use patterned material on the inside of the chair and a dark, matching material on the outside. This last idea is for plain-tailored covers on modern furniture.

Self-patterned material

A self-patterned material is one where the pattern repeats itself so often that it gives an all-over effect – a small check or flower for instance – or a pattern formed from the weaving instead of a combination of colours. Damasks, brocades and woollen weaves are in this last category.

Woollen weaves give covers an expensive, upholstered look. They mould themselves to the chair and cling as if fixed there. Unfortunately, they are expensive.

Self-patterned materials are as economical to use as plain because the pattern does not have to be centred, and their texture makes them a little more interesting than plain materials.

Finishing self-patterned covers. They can be finished in any of the ways given for patterned covers, although a box-pleated frill is preferable to a gathered one. They can also be plain-tailored. If an upholstered effect is required then the cover should obviously be plain-tailored.

Ideas for self-patterned covers. Some manufacturers offer plain woollen materials in four or five colours, together with one check or mixture incorporating all the colours. Any one colour in the plain range will therefore match the check or mixture. Covers made of one of the plain colours, with boxed cushions in the check or mixture, look most attractive.

A good touch with a plain tailored finish is to hand sew fringed braid round the bottom of the cover after it has been sewn up. This is not too effective, however, if there is a large gap between the bottom of the chair and the floor.

All-over pattern

This is a sprawling, sometimes large pattern, so involved that you have to look very hard to see any kind of repeat. Paisley designs are usually all-over, and sometimes Jacobean patterns.

All-over patterns should be treated in the same way as self-patterned materials.

Plain material

Covers of plain material in light colours often look more suited to a waiting room than a home, while dark colours show up every speck of dust as a grey powder. The best course is a happy medium. Note also that crooked seams show up more in plain covers.

On the other hand there is virtually no wastage with plain covers, and they are the easiest to cut and fit. They are at their best on modern furniture with clean, simple lines.

Finishing plain covers. Plain covers can be finished in any of the ways previously mentioned, except that a gathered frill is not apt for this non-fussy material.

Ideas for plain covers. They can be brightened up with plenty of scatter cushions or with contrasting piping.

Some interesting combinations can be obtained with, say, the outside of the chair in a darker shade of the inside and all the piping in the dark material. Another idea is to have boxed cushions in a darker shade of the cover material, with the cover piped in the cushion material and vice versa. These ideas can also be used with contrasting colours.

If you use a combination it must be in shades or colours of the same material; otherwise it will look as if you ran out of one lot of material, were unable to get any more, and patched the cover up with another material. For the same reason you should provide the links suggested with the piping.

2
ESTIMATING

MAIN PIECES FOR CHAIR/SETTEE COVERS

There are at most twelve main pieces to a chair/settee cover, for which only seven sets of measurements have to be taken for estimating and cutting:

1. Inside Back (I/B)
2. Outside Back (O/B)
3. Two Inside Arms (I/A)
4. Two Outside Arms (O/A)
5. Two Inside Wings (I/W)
6. Two Outside Wings (O/W)
7. Two Front Arms (F/A) or Top Arms (T/A)

The main pieces run lengthways down the chair as shown in Figure 7, and it is important to be consistent in this respect. The

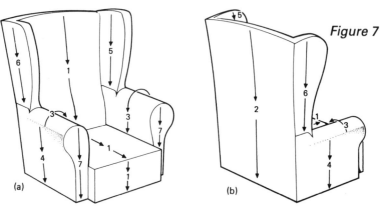

Figure 7

Note that although No. 1 is called the I/B,
this piece extends to the seat and front on armchairs/settees

flowers of a pattern cannot be allowed to grow upside down or sideways and although you can take your choice as to which way is up with a geometrical pattern, it does have to show uniformly on all parts of the chair. Even with a plain material there is the possibility that it may look a different shade from a different angle.

Your only concern when estimating is to provide for pieces wide enough and long enough to cover the parts of the chair for which they are intended. Shape is not important at this stage, since the most intricate part can be reduced to a rectangle (Figure 8).

Figure 8

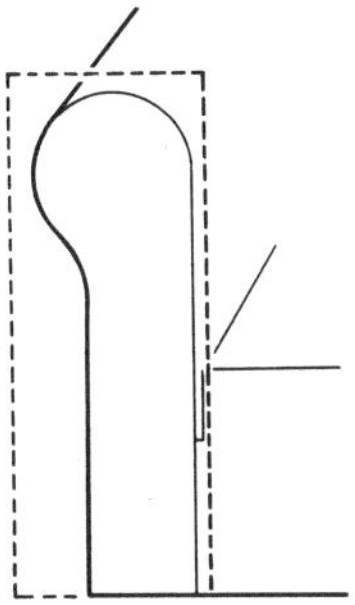

Width

The width measurement is for working out *how many* widths you will need. A chair back up to 22 in (56 cm) wide would require only half a width of 48 in (122 cm) wide material, while one that is more than 22 in (56 cm) wide would require a full width; a settee back might require one, one and a half or even two widths. If more than one similar item is being covered then the number of widths increases accordingly, i.e. for a three-piece suite: two chairs with inside backs more than 22 in (56 cm) wide = two widths. Settee back more than 70 in (178 cm) wide = two widths. Total required for all inside backs = four widths.

The above applies to all the main pieces; inside and outside arms being estimated to the half width or full width, while smaller pieces such as wings, front arms, etc. are estimated to the quarter width or half width.

Incidentally, you can rest assured that you have not given house room to a material-gobbling monster if your chair requires full widths for backs and arms. Most chairs require full widths for these pieces. Also do not be alarmed if full widths are required for parts that are only a few inches too big for half widths.

While it is true that the superfluous material will be trimmed away at the fitting stage, large trimmings can be used for other parts of the cover, frill, flaps and piping.

Figure 9

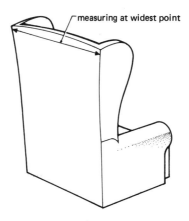

measuring at widest point

It is easy to see that if you measured the width of the outside back in Figure 9 at the bottom instead of the top, and consequently estimated a half width instead of a full width, your estimate would be a great deal short. The proper places to measure are not always so obvious, however. The Figures in the following directions show where different styles are likely to be widest and longest, but you should keep trying with your tape measure until you are sure you have found the widest point on *your* chair.

Length

Since the material must run down the main pieces, the length of each main piece is the *amount* to estimate. Again, keep trying with the tape measure until you are sure that you are measuring at the longest point.

Allowances

The appropriate allowances to add to the width and length measurements are given for each main piece in the following directions. Generally, they are as follows:

Seams. 1 in (2.5 cm) for fitted covers; ⅝ in (1.5 cm) for covers made from measurements, such as boxed cushion covers. These allowances include a little extra in case of shrinkage.

Tuck-seams.   An armchair/settee usually requires only one piece for the inside back, seat and front (called the inside back), which is much easier than measuring, estimating and cutting three or four separate pieces. The piece is divided and shaped at the fitting stage with the aid of tuck-seams (Figure 10a). Two in (5 cm) is allowed for a 1 in (2.5 cm) tuck, which when cut open becomes an ordinary 1 in (2.5 cm) seam (Figure 10b).

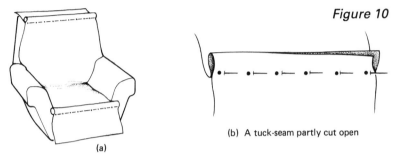

Figure 10

(b) A tuck-seam partly cut open

(a)

Hems.   Allow 2 in (5 cm) for a 1 in (2.5 cm) hem with 1 in (2.5 cm) turned in.

Tuck-in.   This is an extra bit of cover that is tucked into the recesses at the back and sides of the seat, and at the sides of the inside back (Figure 11). Tuck-in prevents the cover from splitting when the chair is sat on and the seat and back are depressed. It also keeps the cover in place.

Figure 11

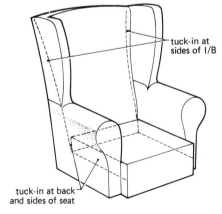

tuck-in at sides of I/B

tuck-in at back and sides of seat

Usually there are no set allowances for tuck-in. Just push the tape well inside the recesses when measuring.

Note that where you are unable to push the tape into a recess, tuck-in allowance is not needed as there is no give at this point when the chair is sat on.

Reserves

Sometimes a full width has to be estimated when only a half width is required, and the other half width cannot be used immediately. In this event the remaining half width should be noted on the estimating list as a reserve, and used up as and when the opportunity occurs either for other pieces, frills, flaps or piping. The overall estimate can then be reduced accordingly.

The occasions when a reserve will arise are noted in the following directions.

Overall estimate

Since it is impossible to estimate with complete accuracy, be generous when allowing extra material for matching a pattern and when rounding off the final figure. Rather have a yard or so over – useful for arm caps, antimacassars, cushions or just for possible future repairs – than a few inches too little and find there is no more material in stock when you want it.

Sample estimating and cutting list

The example opposite is for an average armchair with a boxed cushion. The measurements are not representative of any particular chair, however, and are quoted as an example of method only. Make a similar list and keep it for the cutting stage to save taking the same measurements all over again.

INSIDE AND OUTSIDE BACKS

Measure the width of the I/B where it is widest, add 2 in (5 cm) for seams and enter in column 2 of the estimating list. **Measure** the length of the I/B where it is longest, add the appropriate allowances (see facing list) and enter the total in column 3.

Measure the width of the O/B where it is widest, add 2 in (5 cm) for seams and enter in column 2. **Measure** the length of the O/B where it is longest, add 1 in (2.5 cm) for the seam plus 2 in (5 cm) for the hem if the cover is plain-tailored and enter in column 3.

1	2	3	4	5	6
Item	Width	Length ×	No. of Widths =	Total	Notes
Inside Back	38"	68"	1	68"	
Outside Back	37"	31"	1	31"	
Side Borders to back	11"	17"	1	17"	Reserve 24" × 17"
Inside arms	21"	23"	1	23"	
Outside arms	29"	20"	2	40"	
Front arms	12"	20"	1	20"	Reserve 24" × 20" Total: 24" × 37"
Pleated Frill		8"	5	40"	
Boxed Cushion	21½"	24"	1	24"	
Boxed Cushion Border		4¼"	2	9"	Approx.
Piping: chair		11½ yds ⎫		18"	16 yds required in
Piping: cushion		4½ yds ⎭			all: 14½ from estimated ½ yd, remainder from trimmings
Extra for patterned material				18"	
				308"	
Less reserves: 24" × 37" equal to 48" × 18½", say:				18"	
(Reserves can be used for frill or piping)				290"	= 8 yds 2"

ESTIMATE: 8¼ yards or 7.5 metres

N.B. *REMOVE BOXED CUSHIONS BEFORE ESTIMATING*

	Allowances on Length
Top seam (all types)	1 in (2.5 cm)
Tuck seam at top border, as in Figure 12 b	2 in (5 cm)
Tuck seam at front border or front seat, as in Figure 12g	2 in (5 cm)
Hem if cover has no seat, or is plain-tailored	2 in (5 cm)
Extra if chair does not have a boxed cushion, and a pattern has to be centred on the seat	9 in (23 cm)

Estimate the number of widths required for all items; enter these in column 4 and multiply out to column 5. Estimate as appropriate, according to width plus allowances:

Figure 12

Fireside inside backs   *Alternative places to measure the extent of the I/B*

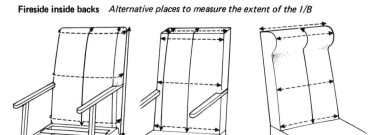

(a)   (b)   (c)

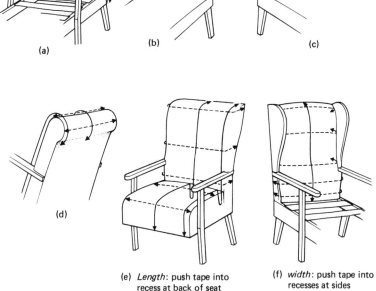

(d)

(e) *Length*: push tape into
     recess at back of seat

(f) *width*: push tape into
     recesses at sides

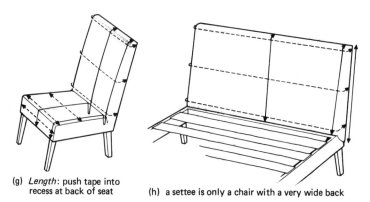

(g) *Length*: push tape into
     recess at back of seat

(h) a settee is only a chair with a very wide back

On (b), (c) and (d) do not include side borders in the width

Figure 13

Armchair inside backs *Alternative places to measure the extent of the I/B*

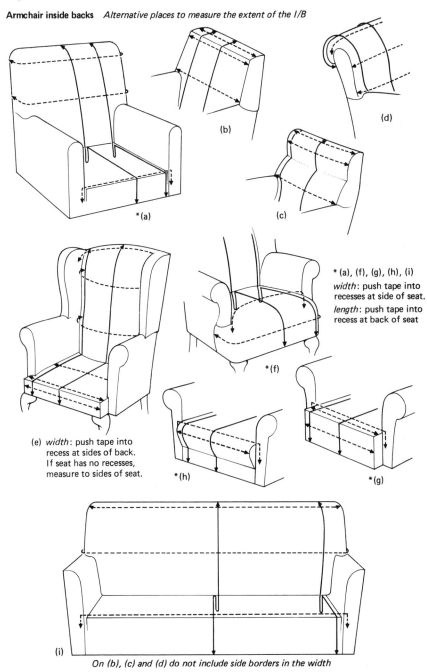

*(a), (f), (g), (h), (i)
width: push tape into recesses at side of seat.
length: push tape into recess at back of seat

(e) *width*: push tape into recess at sides of back. If seat has no recesses, measure to sides of seat.

On (b), (c) and (d) do not include side borders in the width

Figure 14

Fireside outside backs

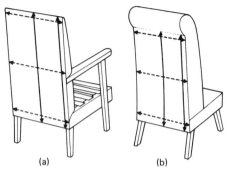

(a)   (b)

(a) shows alternative places to measure for all types except those with back rolls, as in (b)

I/B and O/B up to 24 in (61 cm) wide
1 chair: 1 width × length of longer back. (Length of shorter back for cutting purposes only.)
2 chairs: I/B – 1 width; O/B – 1 width.

I/B up to 24 in (61 cm) wide, O/B more than 24 in (61 cm) wide; or vice versa
1 chair: I/B – 1 width; O/B – 1 width. Reserve a half width × the length of the narrower back.
2 chairs: Narrower back – 1 width; wider back – 2 widths.

I/B and O/B up to 48 in (122 cm) wide
1 chair/settee: I/B – 1 width; O/B – 1 width.
2 chairs: I/B – 2 widths; O/B – 2 widths.

I/B up to 48 in (122 cm) wide, O/B more than 48 in (122 cm) wide; or vice versa
Settee: Narrower back – 1 width; wider back – 2 widths. Reserve a half width × the length of the wider back.

I/B and O/B up to 72 in (183 cm) wide
Settee: Shorter back – 1 width; longer back – 2 widths.

Figure 15

Armchair outside backs

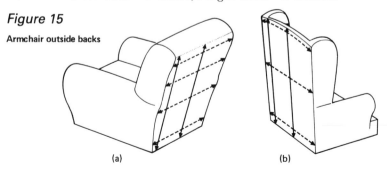

(a)   (b)

alternative places to measure for all types of armchairs, with and without wings

I/B up to 72 in (183 cm) wide, O/B more than 72 in (183 cm) wide; or vice versa

Settee: I/B – 2 widths; O/B – 2 widths. Reserve a half width × the length of the narrower back.

I/B and O/B up to 96 in (244 cm)

Settee: I/B – 2 widths; O/B – 2 widths.

On a three-piece suite, check if the length of the settee back is the same as the chairs. If it is not, estimate the settee separately.

INSIDE AND OUTSIDE ARMS

Estimate for I/As first then O/As in the same manner

Fireside inside and outside arms

Measure the width of the arm where it is widest, add 2 in (5 cm) for seams and enter in column 2 of the list. **Measure** the length of the arm where it is longest, add appropriate allowances (see list, page 34) enter in column 3.

upholstered panel

Figure 16

Alternative places to measure the extent of the I/A and O/A

push the tape into any small recess there may be where the I/A meets the I/B

(a) and (b) include the sides of wooden tops *and/or* fronts in measurements

(a)

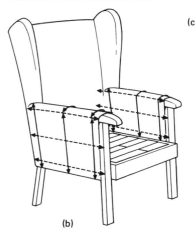

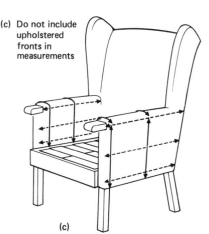

(c) Do not include upholstered fronts in measurements

(b)

(c)

Figure 17

Inside arms   *alternative places to measure the extent of the I/A*

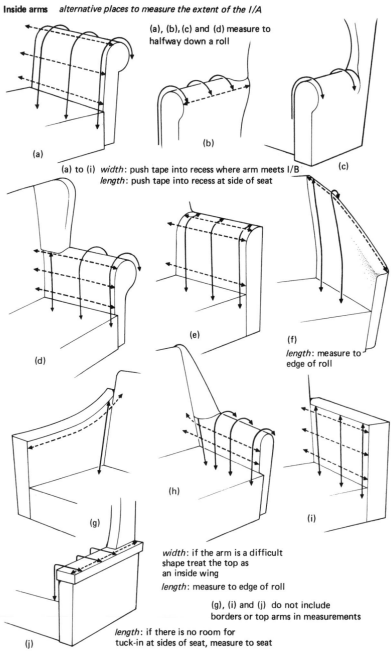

(a), (b), (c) and (d) measure to halfway down a roll

(a)

(b)

(c)

(a) to (i) *width*: push tape into recess where arm meets I/B
        length: push tape into recess at side of seat

(d)

(e)

(f)

length: measure to edge of roll

(g)

(h)

(i)

(j)

width: if the arm is a difficult shape treat the top as an inside wing

length: measure to edge of roll

(g), (i) and (j) do not include borders or top arms in measurements

length: if there is no room for tuck-in at sides of seat, measure to seat

Figure 18

Outside arms
*alternative places to measure
the extent of O/As*

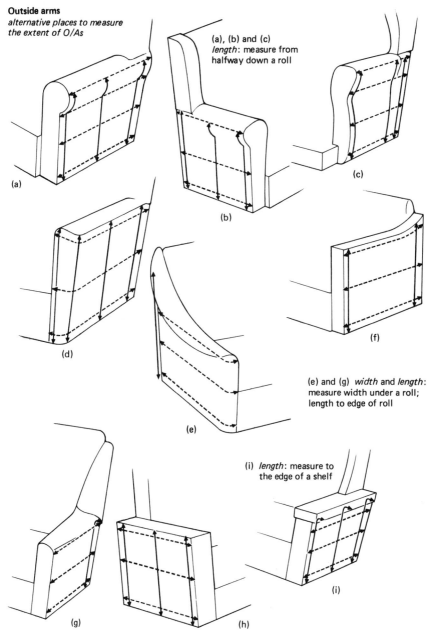

(a), (b) and (c)
length: measure from
halfway down a roll

(a)

(b)

(c)

(d)

(e)

(f)

(e) and (g) *width* and *length*:
measure width under a roll;
length to edge of roll

(g)

(h)

(i) *length*: measure to
the edge of a shelf

(i)

	Allowances on Length
Seam at top (all arms)	1 in (2.5 cm)
Hem on I/As if cover has no seat	2 in (5 cm)
Hem on O/As if cover is plain-tailored	2 in (5 cm)

Estimate the number of widths required for all items as appropriate, according to width plus allowances:

I/A or O/A up to 24 in (61 cm) wide
1 width per chair/settee.

I/A or O/A more than 24 in (61 cm) wide
2 widths per chair/settee.

INSIDE AND OUTSIDE WINGS

Inside wings in patterned material must match the inside back as explained on page 74; consequently, only one pair can be obtained from a width of material regardless of the width of the wing. Outside wings do not have to match the outside back, however, as they are not seen as one with it.

Measure, add allowances and enter width and length in their respective columns for the I/W, then for the O/W. Allowances are the same for inside and outside wings:
Allowances on width: 2 in (5 cm) for seams.
Allowances on length: 2 in (5 cm) for seams, or 1 in (2.5 cm) for seam plus 2 in (5 cm) for hem if the wing is above a wooden arm.

Figure 19

Inside wings   *alternative places to measure the extent of I/Ws*

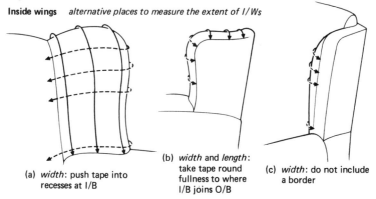

(a) *width*: push tape into recesses at I/B

(b) *width* and *length*: take tape round fullness to where I/B joins O/B

(c) *width*: do not include a border

Figure 20

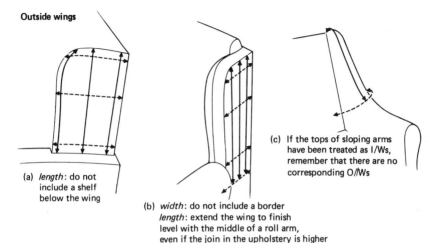

Outside wings

(a) *length*: do not include a shelf below the wing

(b) *width*: do not include a border
length: extend the wing to finish level with the middle of a roll arm, even if the join in the upholstery is higher

(c) If the tops of sloping arms have been treated as I/Ws, remember that there are no corresponding O/Ws

Estimate the number of widths required for all items as appropriate, according to width plus allowances:

I/W and O/W up to 12 in (30 cm) wide, patterned or plain
1 width per chair/settee × the length of the longer wing. (Length of shorter wing for cutting purposes only.)

I/W up to 12 in (30 cm) wide; O/W more than 12 in (30 cm) wide, patterned
I/W – 1 width per chair/settee; O/W 1 width per chair/settee. Reserve a half width × the length of the I/W per chair/settee. (Example: for a wing 10 in (25 cm) wide × 23 in (58 cm) long reserve from 1 chair = 24 × 23 in (61 × 58 cm); 2 chairs = 24 × 46 in (61 × 117 cm); three-piece = 24 × 69 in (61 × 175 cm).

I/W up to 12 in (30 cm) wide; O/W more than 12 in (30 cm) wide, plain
1/W – 1 width for 1* or 2 chairs; 2 widths for 3-piece*.
O/W – 1 width per chair/settee.
*Reserve a half width × the length of the I/W.

I/W more than 12 in (30 cm) wide; O/W up to 12 in (30 cm) wide, patterned or plain
I/W – 1 width per chair/settee.
O/W 1 width for 1* or 2 chairs; 2 widths for 3-piece*.
*Reserve a half width × the length of the O/W.

I/W and O/W more than 12 in (30 cm) wide, patterned or plain
I/W – 1 width per chair/settee.
O/W 1 width per chair/settee.

FRONT ARMS

Before estimating check if small F/As can be covered out of
trimmings, as explained in the Minor Pieces Section, page 38.
Estimate for standard-sized F/As as directed.

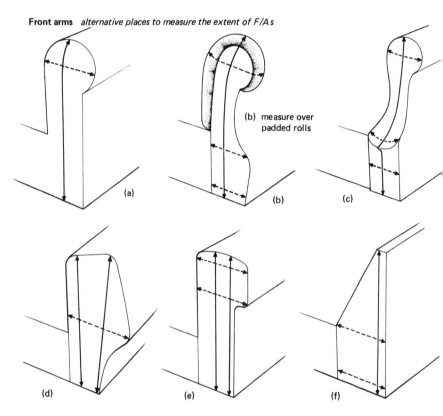

Front arms   *alternative places to measure the extent of F/As*

(b) measure over padded rolls

(a)   (b)   (c)   (d)   (e)   (f)

Figure 21

Note that as these are prominent eye-catching parts of the
chair, F/As in patterned material must match; consequently only
one pair of F/As can be obtained from a width of material.

Measure, add allowances and enter width and length in the respective columns. Allowances to add are:
Width: 2 in (5 cm) for seams.
Length: 1 in (2.5 cm) for seams; or 1 in (2.5 cm) for seam plus 2 in (5 cm) for hem if cover is plain-tailored.

Estimate as appropriate, according to width plus allowances:

F/A up to 12 in (30 cm) wide, patterned
1 width per chair/settee. Reserve half a width × the length of the F/A per chair/settee. (See example of a reserve per chair/settee from wings in the second estimate, page 35.)

F/A up to 12 in (30 cm) wide, plain
1 width for 1* or 2 chairs; 2 widths for a 3-piece.*
*Reserve a half width × the length of the F/A.

F/A up to 24 in (61 cm) wide, plain or patterned
1 width per chair/settee.

TOP ARMS

These long pieces can be estimated and cut more economically from the width of the material, provided that it will not be obvious that a pattern is running sideways or that one T/A does not match the other.

Figure 22

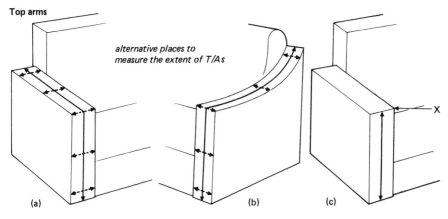

Top arms

alternative places to
measure the extent of T/As

X

(a)   (b)   (c)

If it will be noticeable that a pattern is running the wrong way, or that the arms do not match, estimate and cut same as for F/As on the previous page; if not, estimate as follows:

Measure *length* where T/A is longest, add 1 in (2.5 cm) for seams or 1 in (2.5 cm) for seam plus 2 in (5 cm) for hem if the cover is plain-tailored, and enter in column *2* of list.

Measure *width* where T/A is widest, add 2 in (5 cm) for seams and enter in column *3*.

Estimate as appropriate, according to width plus allowance:

T/As up to 48 in (122 cm) long.　(Column 2) – 2 widths per chair/settee.

T/As more than 48 in (122 cm) long.　(Column 2) – each T/A will require two pieces joining at point X on Figure 22c; therefore estimate 2 widths per chair/settee for the tops plus:

1 width for fronts up to 23 in (58 cm) long (21 in (53 cm) if plain-tailored);
2 widths for fronts more than 23 in (58 cm) long (21 in (53 cm) if plain-tailored).

MINOR PIECES

Generally the minor, or smaller pieces of armchairs/settees can be covered out of trimmings from the main pieces, but if the minor pieces are fairly large then it is best to check if there will be enough suitable material left. Particularly check what trimmings will be available from smaller chairs, since these estimates can be so economical – i.e. all the main pieces obtained from half-widths – that there will be no trimmings to speak of.

To ascertain what trimmings are available simply deduct the width required for a main piece from the width of the material and divide by two; e.g. if a width has been estimated for a piece 30 in wide × 31 in (76 × 79 cm) long there will be two trimmings (one from each side of the piece) 31 in (76 cm) long and at least 9 in (22 cm) wide.

If there are no suitable trimmings measure and estimate as follows:

TV and fireside chairs

Vertical Borders (estimated from width of material). Figure 23a, b and c. Width: add 2 in (5 cm) for seams (enter in column 3). *Length:* add 2 in (5 cm) for seams, or 1 in (2.5 cm) for seam plus 2 in (5 cm) for a hem (enter in column 2).

Figure 23

Borders on TV and fireside chairs   *alternative places to measure the extent of borders*

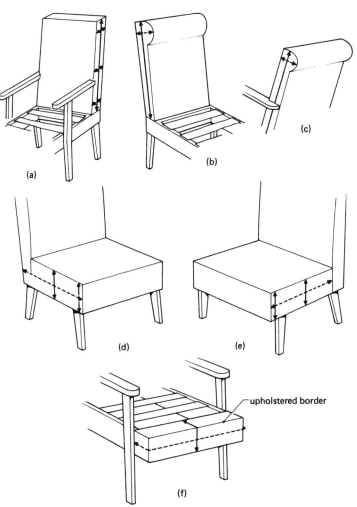

(a)

(b)

(c)

(d)

(e)

upholstered border

(f)

Estimate: 1 width per pair up to 24 in (61 cm) long including allowances (column 2); 2 widths per pair if more than 24 in (61 cm) long including allowances (column 2).

Horizontal borders. Figure 23d, e and f.   Width: add 2 in (5 cm) for seams. *Length:* add 1 in (2.5 cm) for seam, plus 2 in (5 cm) for a hem. *Estimate* for chairs as in Figure 23d and e: 1 width per pair up to 24 in (61 cm) wide including allowances; 2 widths per pair if more than 24 in (61 cm) wide including allowances. *Estimate* for chairs as in Figure 23f: 1 width.

If seat has upholstered borders at the sides, estimate the same as for Figure 23d or e.

Armchairs/settees

Side borders on back. Figure 24a.   *Width and Length*: add 2 in (5 cm) for seams. *Estimate*: 1 width for a chair, settee or 2 chairs; 2 widths for a 3-piece.

Figure 24

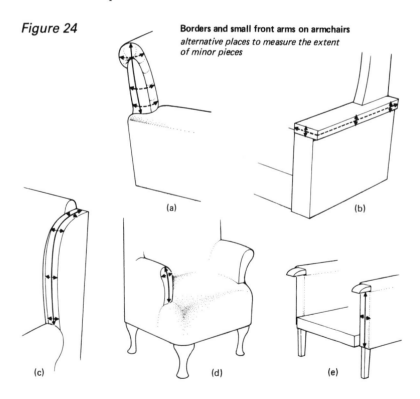

Borders and small front arms on armchairs
alternative places to measure the extent of minor pieces

(a)

(b)

(c)

(d)

(e)

Borders on arms. Figure 24b.   *Width and Length*: add 2 in (5 cm) for seams. *Estimate*: 2 widths per chair/settee.

Borders on wings. Figure 24c.   *Width and Length*: add 2 in (5 cm) for seams. *Estimate* from the width of the material, as for vertical borders on TV and fireside chairs, above.

Small front arms. Figure 24d.   If these cannot be covered from trimmings estimate the same as for standard F/As, page 37.

Front arm borders. Figure 24e.   Width: add 2 in (5 cm) for seams. *Length*: add 1 in (2.5 cm) for seam, plus 2 in (5 cm) for a hem. *Estimate* from the width of the material as for vertical borders.

Flaps for plain-tailored covers

Four pieces 12 × 6 in (30 × 15 cm) are required per chair; two pieces 24 × 6 in (61 × 15 cm) and two pieces 12 × 6 in (30 × 15 cm) per settee. If there are no suitable trimmings estimate 6 in (30 cm) in column 3; 1 width per chair and 2 widths per settee in column 4.

SKIRTS AND FRILLS

The length of the finished skirt or frill should be 6–8 in (15–20 cm); but if the chair is high at the front and slopes towards the back, the finished length of the frill should be the length from the front to the floor. If the bottom of the chair is more than 8 in (20 cm) from the floor the chair would probably look better in a plain-tailored cover.

Choose the length you require (6 in (15 cm) is recommended), add ½ in (1.25 cm) for the seam and 1½ in (4 cm) for the hem, and enter in column 3 of your list.

Skirt with corner pleats

Enter in column 4 of list: 4 widths per chair; 6 widths per settee.

Plain skirt in four panels – one each at front, back and sides

Measure the width of the front at the level the skirt will start, add 3 in (7.5 cm) for side hems and **estimate** as appropriate for the front and back; **measure** one side at the same level, add 3 in (7.5 cm) for side hems and **estimate** for the sides as appropriate.

Enter the total number of widths in column 4 or your list as follows:

	Front and Back				Sides	
	Width, including allowances, up to:					
	24 in (61 cm)	48 in (122 cm)	72 in (183 cm)	96 in (244 cm)	24 in (61 cm)	48 in (122 cm)
No. of widths per chair/settee:	1	2	3	4	1	2

Frill

Measure all round the width of the chair/settee at about the level at which the frill will start and add allowances as follows:
1½ × all-round width for gathers
2 × all-round width for 2 in (5 cm) pleats with 2 in (5 cm) spaces between.
Divide the all-round width by 48 in (122 cm) to work out the number of widths required, and enter the greatest whole number in column 4 of your list.

Examples for an all-round width of 90 in (229 cm)

Gathers: 1½ × 90 in (229 cm) = 135 in (343 cm) ÷ by 48 in (122 cm) = 2 widths and 39 in (99 cm) = 3 widths.

Pleats: 2 × 90 in (229 cm) = 180 in (457 cm) ÷ by 48 in (122 cm) = 3 widths and 36 in (91 cm) = 4 widths.

Reserves

Small reserves are more suitable for piping than for frill.

To estimate how much frill a large reserve will make divide the length of the reserve by the length plus allowances of the frill; then, as the answer will be in half widths (because the reserve is a half width), divide by two to convert to widths.

Example of a reserve 24 in wide × 65 in long (61 × 165 cm) for a frill 6 in (15 cm) long plus 2 in (5 cm) allowances:
65 in (165 cm) ÷ by 8 in (20 cm) = 8 half widths = 4 widths.
Deduct 4 widths from the estimate for frill.

CHAIR, SETTEE AND DIVAN CUSHIONS

If cushions only are being covered, read the general directions for estimating chair covers, pages 22–6 many of which apply to cushions.

Check that all cushions are the same size and estimate separately for different sizes. Remember that the two outside cushions of a three-seater settee are often wider than the middle one.

Figure 25

Chair, settee and divan cushions *alternative places to measure the extent of pieces*

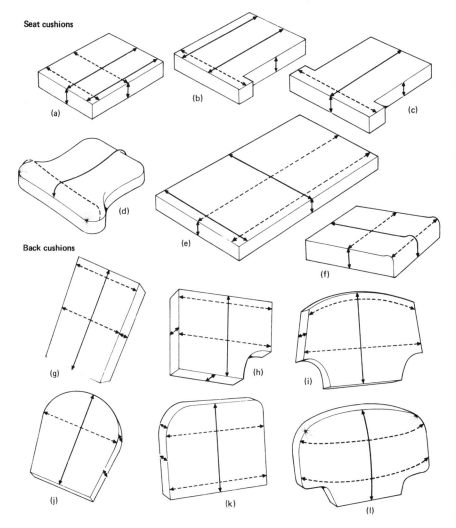

Tops and bottoms

Measure the top where it is widest and longest, add 1¼ in (3 cm) for seams in each case, and enter in columns 2 and 3 respectively.
Estimate the appropriate number of widths in column 4 and multiply out to column 5:

	Width, including allowances, up to:			
No. of widths per:	24 in (61 cm)	48 in (122 cm)	72 in (183 cm)	96 in (244 cm)
chair/settee/divan cushion:	1	2	3	4

Borders for boxed cushions

Measure the border where it is longest, add 1¼ in (3 cm) for seams and enter in column 3 of your list. **Estimate** as appropriate:

	Width, including allowances, up to:			
No. of widths per:	24 in (61 cm)	48 in (122 cm)	72 in (183 cm)	96 in (244 cm)
All-round border, chair/settee cushion:	2	3		
Divan cushion:		4	5	6
Part border, chair/settee cushion (Figure 25f):	1	1		

Openings

If covering cushions only, and the estimate has been economical – i.e. half widths for tops and bottoms – estimate for openings: 1 width per chair/settee cushion; 2 widths per divan cushion.

Sample estimate.   Boxed cushion 20 in wide × 21½ in long (51 × 55 cm) with 3 in (7.5 cm) long borders:
Top and bottom 1 width × 22¾ in, say 23 in (58 cm). Border 2 widths × 4¼ (11 cm) = 8½ in, say 9 in (22 cm).

PIPING

Estimate the amount of piping required per chair/settee by adding the measurements of the piped seams together as in the following example:

Chair/settee cover. Figure 26.

Top and sides of O/B (A) – (B)
O/A × 2 (C) – (D)
F/A × 2 (E) – (F)
Seat front (G) – (H)
Wings × 2 (I) – (J)
Base of frilled cover (K) – (L)
Any other place where the upholstery is piped, e.g. (Y) – (Z)

Figure 26

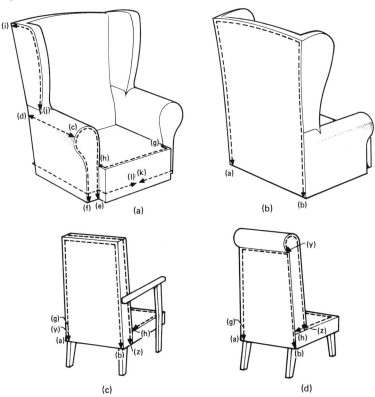

Cushions. Figure 27.

With side borders 2 × (Y) − (Z), diagram (a)
Borders all round 2 × all-round width diagram (b)
Without border 1 × all-round width diagram (c)

Figure 27

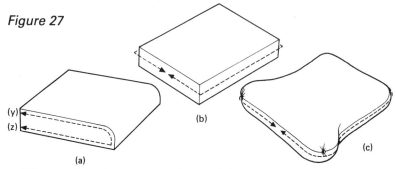

(y)

(z)

(b)

(c)

(a)

The total is the amount for which you require material for casing. Brought to the greatest number of yards/metres it is also the amount of piping cord required (see Extras, page 47).

Estimate the amount of material required on the basis that 1 yd × 48 in (122 cm)-wide material will make about 30 yds (27 metres) of piping. Bring the estimate to the nearest ¼ yd (25 cm) and enter in column 3 of your list.

Example: 12 yards (11 metres) of piping required: estimate ½ yd (50 cm) material

Trimmings

If there are trimmings, i.e. if the main pieces have generally required full widths, it is probably safe to say that 1–1½ yds (1–1.5 metres) of material are sufficient for casing the piping for an average three-piece suite and its boxed cushions, even though this will provide only about half the amount required, because the remainder can be made up from trimmings. As you go down the scale of the number of items to be covered and their size, the less trimmings will be available and the more exact your estimate will need to be, however.

In the example on page 27 it was established that 16 yds (14.5 metres) of piping would be required in all, but only ½ yd of material was estimated for piping because full widths were estimated for several pieces of the chair cover, and there would be trimmings from these pieces.

Reserves

Deduct half the length of any reserve you wish to use for piping. (A piece 24 × 18 in (61 × 46 cm) will make near enough the same amount of piping as a piece 48 × 9 in (122 × 23 cm) because the area is the same.)

EXTRAS

Cotton thread to match the material	Approx. 4 reels per chair; 6 reels per settee
Odd cottons in various colours for tacking	
Piping cord, size 3, pre-shrunk; or shrink by boiling	As measured on pages 45–6
½ in (1.25 cm) tape, black or white as suitable:	
Plain tailored covers:	Chair: 2 yds (2 metres); settee 3 yds (3 metres), approximately
With frill or skirt:	2 yds (2 metres) per chair/settee, approximately
Fastenings for openings on chair/settee covers, cushion covers, etc. Three kinds are suitable:	The size of the opening cannot be determined until the fitting stage
Hooks and bars size 4 (tedious to sew by hand but inexpensive)	A pair every 2 in (5 cm) of opening
Hook and eyelet tape by the yard/metre (sewn by machine and gives a good, firm finish)	Extent of opening plus 1 in (2.5 cm)
Heavy duty zipper (easiest to sew but quite expensive)	Extent of opening

3
CUTTING AND PLACING

You should have the room to yourself or at least work well out of the way of passers-by. The pins used to secure the material to the chair can inflict vicious wounds and are especially dangerous to children. Also, since the object is to tailor a perfect fit you cannot have people brushing past disturbing the pieces, much less sitting on the furniture while the fitting is in progress.

Prepare the items to be covered by removing any boxed cushions and marking with tailor's chalk the centre of the following parts: I/B at top; upholstered seat at front and at bottom of front; I/As, O/As and O/B at top and bottom (Figure 28).

Straighten one end of the material (the end at the top of a pattern) by trimming along a pulled thread, and work from this end only. It does not matter if the straight of a pattern does not coincide with the pulled thread as the important thing is to cut on the straight of the weave.

Figure 28

(a)   (b)

Measure the length required (column 3 of your chart) at the selvedge and cut at this point across the whole width unless otherwise directed. Cut along a pulled thread or by snipping the selvedge and tearing. Where more than one width is required in column 4, continue measuring and cutting as before until you have the requisite number of widths.

To centre and match a pattern, find the starting point for each width before measuring and cutting as described above. The directions show how to find the starting point for each main piece.

If possible place all the widths as soon as cut. If it is inconvenient to have all the items of a three-piece suite out of commission at the same time, place the first width on a chair as soon as cut; then cut, label and put aside the remainder for each main piece. Continue making the chair cover and put the finished cover on the chair as a model for placing the pieces on the next item to be fitted, and so on.

When putting aside pieces of plain material mark the wrong side if difficult to tell from the front, and mark the top of each piece if the material looks a different shade or texture upside down.

Placing does not mean just draping the pieces on the chair. It means pinning them straight with any pattern centred and semi-fitting them. Use as few pins as possible to anchor the material firmly to the chair, as they will have to be taken out again when the pieces are pinned together.

Place the pieces right side out. Were they to be fitted wrong side out, the left-hand side of the finished cover would end up on the right-hand side of the chair.

There are a few terms in this section that will keep on cropping up:

Pin up a hem if necessary:　Pin up the hems of plain-tailored covers on the wrong side of the material, ready for sewing, before placing the pieces on the chair. Pin a 1 in (2.5 cm) hem with 1 in (2.5 cm) turned in. Follow the straight of a pattern as far as possible, adjusting the amount turned in if this is necessary to keep the pattern straight.

Centre-to-centre:　Match the centre of the material to the centre marked on the chair; or pin two pieces together with centres matching and pin from centre out to sides.

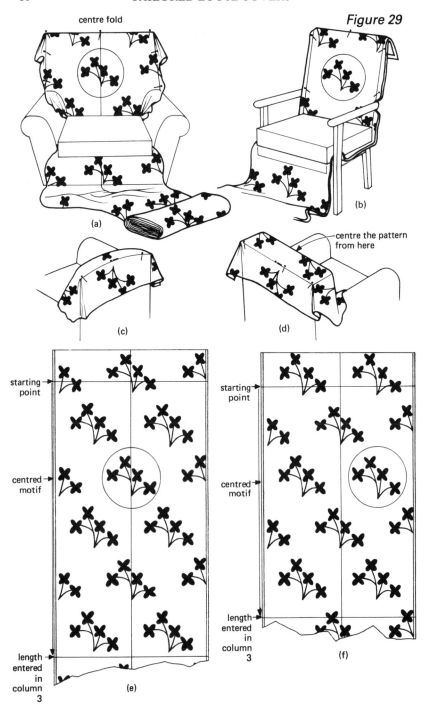

Figure 29

(a)

(b)

(c)

(d)

centre the pattern from here

starting point

centred motif

length entered in column 3

(e)

starting point

centred motif

length entered in column 3

(f)

centre fold

Trim allowances: Trim off any large pieces of unwanted material that will get in the way of the fitting. Do not trim to less than an inch.

Cut and snip: When cutting round a curve the material will ruck up and strain away from the line of shaping, causing you to cut too far. This disaster can easily be avoided by cutting away a little at a time and easing as follows: cut a little, allowing for seam, then snip into the allowance almost to the line of shaping to ease the material flat; cut a little more, and snip, and so on.

INSIDE BACKS

Centring a pattern

Chairs with boxed cushions.   Drape the material on the chair centre-to-centre if a full width is to be placed (Figure 29a), or folded if a half width (Figure 29b). Adjust until the main motif is central between the top of the back and the top of the boxed cushion (put in place temporarily). Smooth the slack to the top and sides and pin the material in place. Tuck the sides in lightly on chairs with wings or sloping arms. Stand back to judge the effect. When you are satisfied that the motif is well shown, mark with a pin the top of the back where it is longest (Figure 29c or d).

Take the material off the chair, open it out if folded, and cut *above* the pin to include allowances as appropriate: 1 in (2.5 cm) for the seam at the top and 2 in (5 cm) for a tuck-seam if there is a top border.

This is the starting point for cutting the centred width. Measure at the selvedge the length entered in column 3 or your list and cut. Figure 29e shows the motif centred on the full width; Figure 29f shows it on the half width.

Chairs without boxed cushions.   Centre the main motif on the back between the top and the seat, following the directions above as far as marking the top of the back where it is longest (Figure 29c or d).

Centre the main motif on the seat, at the same time allowing for tuck-in for the recess at the back of the seat. If there is not enough for tuck-in, centre the next motif down even if this gives too much. (An extra 9 in (23 cm) was estimated in case the

Figure 30

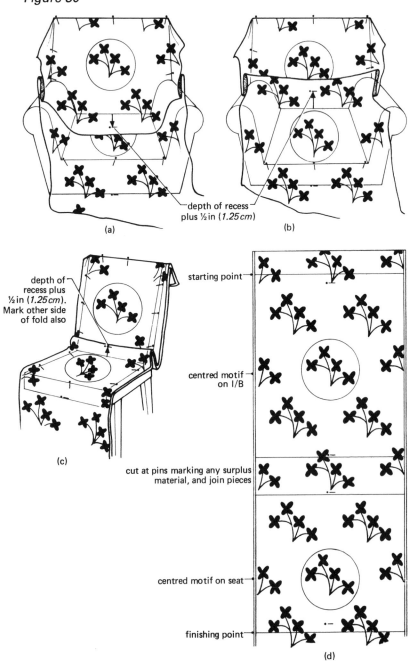

depth of recess
plus ½in (*1.25cm*)

(a)   (b)

depth of
recess plus
½in (*1.25cm*).
Mark other side
of fold also

(c)

starting point

centred motif
on I/B

cut at pins marking any surplus
material, and join pieces

centred motif on seat

finishing point

(d)

pattern did not fall right for the back and seat.) Pin the seat in place at the front.

If there is too much material at the back of the seat to be tucked away, mark where it is to be cut out as follows: Measure the depth of the recess and add ½ in (1.25 cm). Fold the material down and measure this amount from the bottom of the I/B (Figure 30a); fold the material up and measure the same amount from the seat up (Figure 30b). Mark excess material on half widths in the same way (Figure 30c).

After centring the pattern on the seat it is unlikely that the length required will be exactly as estimated in column 3 of your list, so now disregard the estimated length and mark the material with a pin at the bottom of the front.

Remove the material, open it out if folded, and cut *above* the top pin to include allowances as appropriate: 1 in (2.5 cm) for the seam at the top and 2 in (5 cm) for the tuck-seam if there is a top border. This is the starting point of the width.

Dispose of any surplus tuck-in material by cutting at the pins. Pin the seat to the back taking up a ½ in (1.25 cm) seam.

Cut *below* the bottom pin to include allowances as appropriate: 2 in (5 cm) for the tuck-seam at the front of the seat and 2 in (5 cm) for a hem if the cover is plain-tailored.

You now have either one whole piece, or two pieces pinned together, with the motif centred on the back and on the seat (Figure 30d).

Matching a pattern on further widths

The starting point of the centred width is also the matching point for any further widths to be cut for inside backs. Identify the part of the pattern involved at the selvedge, cut off whatever surplus material there may be, then measure and cut the length required. Repeat the procedure until you have the number of widths entered in column 4 of your list (Figure 31).

Beginners might prefer to lay the material on the floor and place the centred width on top with the pattern matching at top and bottom, although this method is tedious if several widths have to be cut.

The strips of material removed (cut out for matching) will themselves match, and should be put aside for front borders on boxed cushions or the front parts of a skirt or frill, depending on the length of the strips.

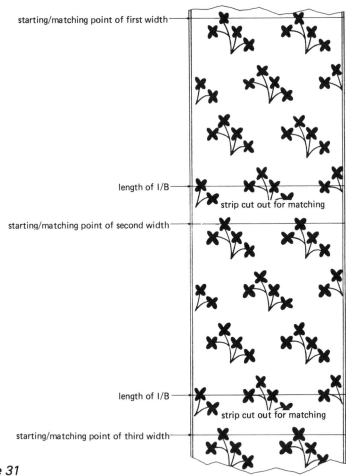

starting/matching point of first width

length of I/B

strip cut out for matching

starting/matching point of second width

length of I/B

strip cut out for matching

starting/matching point of third width

Figure 31

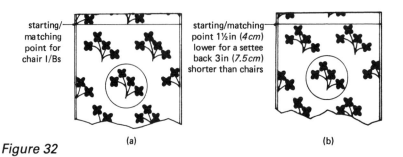

starting/matching point for chair I/Bs

starting/matching point 1½in (*4cm*) lower for a settee back 3in (*7.5cm*) shorter than chairs

(a)

(b)

Figure 32

Chairs without boxed cushions. Where surplus material has been cut out in order to centre a pattern on the seat, label the back and seat lengths before unpinning for cutting further widths. Pin the two pieces of each width together as soon as cut.

Three-piece, settee back a different length from the chairs. Cut and centre the settee back separately from the chairs. Measure the difference from the top to the seat, and raise or lower the matching point by half that difference. If, for instance, a settee back is 3 in (7.5 cm) shorter than the chairs, lower the matching point by 1½ in (4 cm) and cut the length required for the settee back (Figure 32a and b).

CUTTING AND ASSEMBLING WIDTHS

Half-width backs for chairs

Cut the width at the centre fold and place as follows:

One chair, half-width inside and outside back. As the longer back was estimated for, trim one half width to the correct length for the shorter back (Figure 33a), keeping the motif of a pattern central. Place as appropriate.

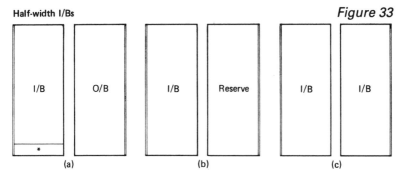

Half-width I/Bs   *Figure 33*

| I/B | O/B | I/B | Reserve | I/B | I/B |

(a)   (b)   (c)

* Trim one half width to length of shorter back, inside or outside as appropriate.
Trim a patterned material at top and/or bottom as necessary to keep the main motif central

One chair, half-width inside back only. Place one half width. Label the other 'reserve' and put aside (Figure 33b).

Two chairs. Place a half width on each inside back (Figure 33c).

One-and-a-half-width or two-width settee backs

A cover must not have a seam running down the centre of an inside or outside back. The one exception is when the upholstery of an inside back is piped down the middle, in which case the two widths are joined at the centre.

One-and-a-half-width I/B

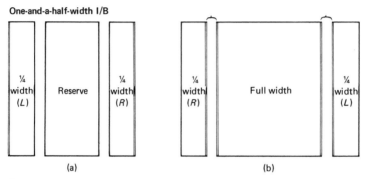

(a)　　　　　　　　　　　　　　(b)

Figure 34

One and a half-width back. Cut a quarter width from each side of a width and reserve the middle (Figure 34a). Pin the quarter widths to the full width, selvedge-to-selvedge (Figure 34b). If the outside back also requires 1½ widths, cut the reserve into quarter widths and trim them to the length of the outside back (assuming it is shorter).

Two-width back. Cut a width into half widths (Figure 35a) and pin it to the full width, selvedge-to-selvedge (Figure 35b).

Two-width I/B

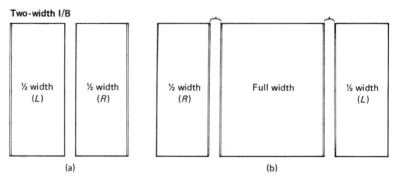

(a)　　　　　　　　　　　　　　(b)

Figure 35

Pinning selvedge-to-selvedge

On the right side, turn under the selvedge of the part width and place it over the selvedge of the full width, with any pattern matching. Insert the pin at the very edge of the fold and pin through all thicknesses.

It is important to keep the pieces at an even tension when pinning. One piece usually ends up longer than the other in any case, because the straight of the material is hardly ever true, so it is hard to tell when a piece is being pulled too taut – until the cover is on the chair, when it is all too obvious.

With a patterned material there is no problem, as by matching the pattern you automatically pin at the correct tension. Choose a distinctive part of the pattern that extends across the seam, and pin wherever it repeats. Still matching the pattern, fill in by pinning at the centre of each gap (Figure 36a). Continue filling in until there are pins every 4–5 in (10–12 cm) (Figure 36b).

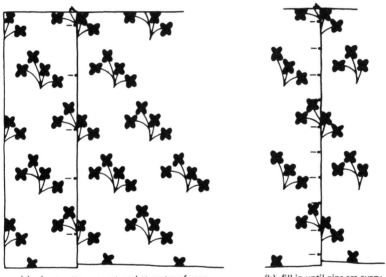

(a) pin at pattern repeat, and at centre of gaps   (b) fill in until pins are every 4-5in (*10-12.5cm*)

Figure 36

Lay pieces of plain material in position, smooth and adjust so that they are as even as possible, and pin at centre, top and bottom. Fill in as for patterned material.

The top and/or bottom of the assembled piece will probably be a little uneven at the joins no matter how well you pin, but there is usually no need to trim them straight. If turning up a bottom hem follow the pattern and lose the unevenness inside the hem.

PLACING INSIDE BACKS

Fireside Backs

Pin up a bottom hem (Figure 37a to 37j). Pin the bottom of the piece to the bottom of the I/B, centre-to-centre, then draw up and pin to the top, centre-to-centre. Smooth out to the sides and pin in place all round. Proceed as appropriate:

Basic.   Pin darts at the top corners. Trim the sides (Figure 37a).

With top border.   Pin a 1 in (2.5 cm) tuck at centre front of the border and pin the border to the back and sides, ensuring that there is enough for seams all round (Figure 37b). Pin the rest of the tuck-seam, taking up any slack due to fullness or the shape of the back. Cut the tuck-seam open (Figure 37c).

With side borders.   Trim the sides after pinning (Figure 37d and e).

With wooden arms.   Fold the side against the arm and at mid-arm level slash the cloth almost to the fold. Keep the fold close to the arm or you will cut too far. Take the I/B round to the O/B, cutting and snipping turnings round the arms (Figure 37f). Pin the turnings to the cover (Figure 37g) and trim the sides.

With upholstered arms (including upholstered arms with wooden tops).   Fold the sides close to the tops of the arms and slash to within 1 in (2.5 cm) of the fold (Figure 37h). Keep the fold close to the arm and slash straight down, or you will cut too far. Take the I/B round to the O/B, cutting and snipping over the arms. Allow for seams over the arms and snip almost to the seam line. Trim the sides above the arms, then trim from the top of the arm to the seat, sharply increasing the allowance to allow for a tuck-in if there is a recess.

With wings and wooden arms.   Slash at the middle of the arm as shown in Figure 37f. Trim the sides from the top to the slash,

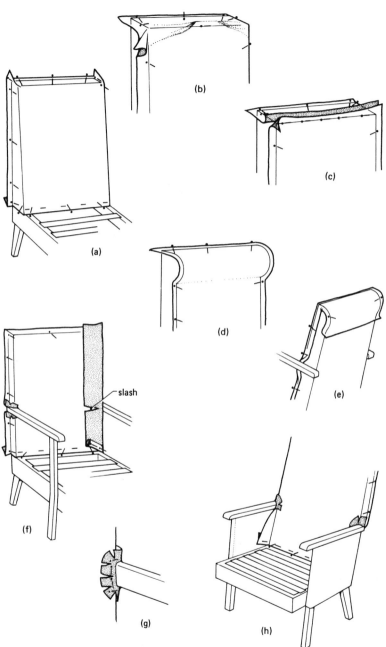

slash

(a) (b) (c) (d) (e) (f) (g) (h)

Figure 37

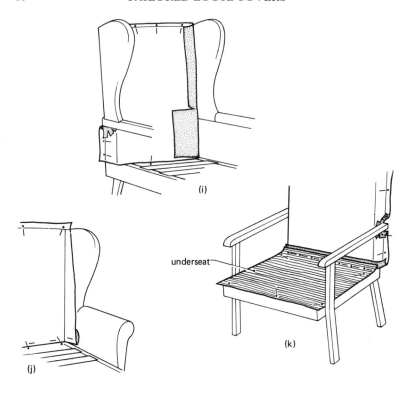

Figure 37 (continued)

allowing for a seam at the top and increasing sharply to as much as possible for the tuck-in. Take the piece round to the O/B below the arms, cutting and snipping turnings beneath arms as shown in Figure 37i. Pin the turnings to the cover. Trim the sides below the arms.

With wings and upholstered arms. Trim the sides allowing for a seam at the top, increasing sharply to as much as possible for the tuck-in (Figure 37j).

Upholstered border below a boxed cushion. Place the back as appropriate then pin an underseat to the bottom of the back (Figure 37k). The underseat should be of a firm material such as curtain lining, the size of the seat plus 1 in (2.5 cm) for a seam all round. The border will be sewn to the underseat.

Armchair/TV chair back and seat

Pin the piece to the I/B centre-to-centre, allowing for a seam at the top and for a tuck-seam if there is a top border. Smooth the slack out to top and sides and pin in place all round. Pin a tuck-seam for a top border as shown for fireside backs (in Figure 37b and c).

Pin up a bottom hem if necessary and pin the bottom of the piece to the bottom of the front, centre-to-centre. Draw up and smooth the material towards the back of the seat. Pin the piece to the sides of the front (Figure 38a) or front border (Figure 38b).

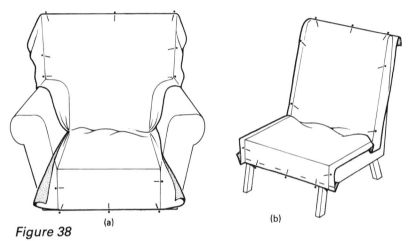

(a) (b)

Figure 38

TV seat and front border. Pin a 1 in (2.5 cm) tuck at the centre front of the seat, straighten the seat cover and pin it to the chair at the sides near the front (Figure 39a). Pin the rest of the tuck-seam, taking up any slack due to shape, and cut the tuck-seam open. Trim the sides of the seat as necessary, allowing for seams, as far as the back of the seat (Figure 39b).

Push the tuck-in inside the back of the seat and trim to the seam allowance at each side. The tuck-in should almost reach the bottom of the recess at the side (Figure 39c). If there is too much material pull it out and adjust with short darts (Figure 39d).

If the back of the chair does not have a side border snip carefully almost to the line of the shaping at the bottom of the tuck-in, take the I/B round to the O/B and trim, allowing for a seam (Figure 39e).

Armchair seat and front.   Pin a 1 in (2.5 cm) tuck at the centre front of the seat, straighten the seat and pin the sides near the front as shown in Figure 39a. Pin the rest of the tuck-seam from arm to arm, taking up any slack due to shape. Cut the tuck-seam open from the centre out to the arms; then continue the cut from the arm across the remainder of the width each side, following a pulled thread.

Fold over the sides of the seat and trim to 4 in (10 cm) for the tuck-in, keeping the folds close to the arms to maintain shape. Do not trim the sides of the front for the time being (Figure 39f).

Figure 39

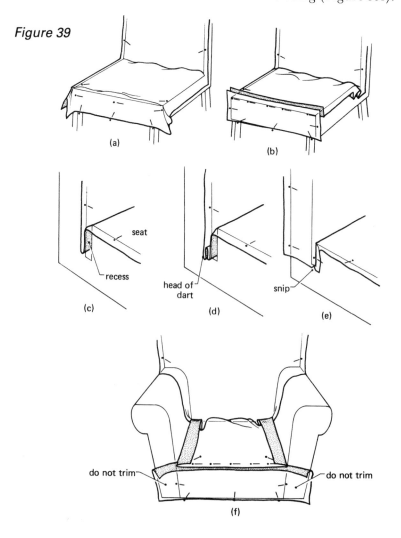

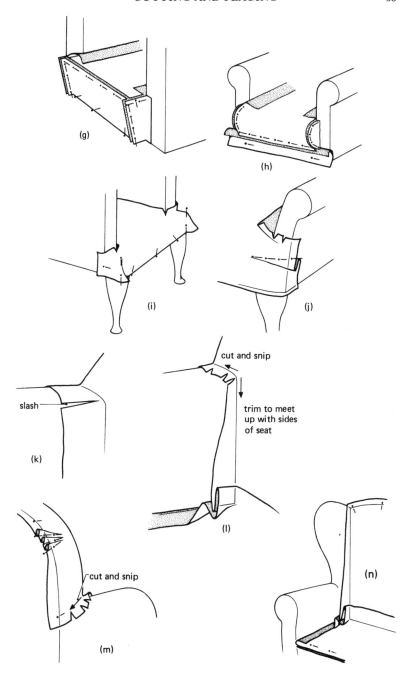

(g)

(h)

(i)

(j)

slash

(k)

cut and snip

trim to meet
up with sides
of seat

(l)

cut and snip

(m)

(n)

With protruding seat.   If the front protrudes more than about 1 in
(2.5 cm) the cover will not sit properly unless the sides are fitted
as separate pieces. Trim the sides of the front, allowing for
seams. Fit the sides from trimmings (off the front, if large
enough), pinning up hems as necessary (Figure 39g or h).

Seat and front in one.   Pin darts at the sides as necessary to dispose
of fullness. Cut and snip to shape round the arms, allowing for a
seam (snip almost to the line of shaping but no farther, as the
latter will be the seam line). At the inside of the arms: either trim
the sides of the seat to the seam allowance (Figure 39i) as tuck-in
is not usually necessary on this type of seat; or sharply increase
the allowance (Figure 39j) to as much as possible, up to 4 in (10
cm). Fold and trim the sides of the seat as shown in Figure 39f.

With shaping over arms.   Slash parallel with the arm to within an
inch of the curve at the inside of the arm (Figure 39k). Trim from
the curve down to the seat, increasing the allowance sharply for
tuck-in. Cut to meet up with the trimmed sides of the seat. Cut
and snip from the curve to the outside of the arm, snipping
carefully almost to line of shaping but no farther, as this will be
the seam line (Figure 39l).
   If the piece has to be taken round to the O/B cut and snip as
before. Fit short darts at the corners of the I/B to dispose of
fullness (Figure 39m).

With wings or sloping arms.   Trim from the top to the seat, allowing 1 in (2.5 cm) at top, increasing sharply for tuck-in. Cut to
meet up with the trimmed sides of the seat (Figure 39n).

OUTSIDE BACKS

Centring a pattern

Measure the length of the back at the centre, from the top to the
level at which a frill or skirt will start (Figure 40a), or from top to
bottom for a plain-tailored cover (Figure 40b). Measure half this
amount up from the centre of the main motif and mark with a
pin. Cut 1 in (2.5 cm) *above* the pin, this being the starting point
for the centred width. Measure at the selvedge the length entered
in column 3 of your list and cut. Figure 40c shows the motif

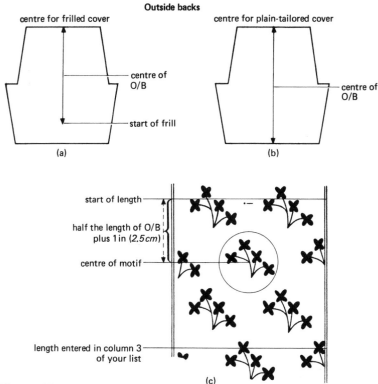

Outside backs

centre for frilled cover

centre of O/B

start of frill

(a)

centre for plain-tailored cover

centre of O/B

(b)

start of length

half the length of O/B plus 1 in (2.5cm)

centre of motif

length entered in column 3 of your list

(c)

Figure 40

centred on a full width, but the method is the same for a half-width piece (see Figure 29f).

Matching a pattern on further widths

Identify the starting point of the centred width at the selvedge and cut each further width to match as shown for I/Bs, (Figure 31). Cut until you have the number of widths entered in column 4 of your list.

Cutting and assembling widths

Follow the same procedure as for I/Bs, page 55.

Placing

Pin up a hem if necessary. Pin the bottom of the piece to the bottom of the back, centre-to-centre, then draw it up and pin to

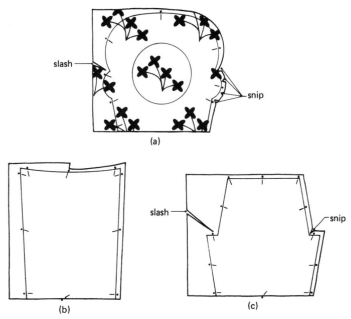

Figure 41

the top, centre-to-centre. Pin at the sides. Where there is an outside roll, pin directly underneath at the sides, keeping the piece taut.

Slash diagonally into corners to within 1 in (2.5 cm) of the line of shaping. Cut and snip round curves, snipping almost to the line of shaping but no farther as this will be the seam line (Figure 41a, b and c).

INSIDE ARMS

Centring a pattern

Drape the material on the arm, centre the main motif, and mark with a pin where the arm is longest, in the same way as for the inside back. Check with Figures 16 and 17 to refresh your memory as to the extent of the inside arm, as the longest part can be in such a variety of places.

Figure 42a shows a full width being centred on the inside arm, and Figure 42b shows the material folded for centring a half-width piece.

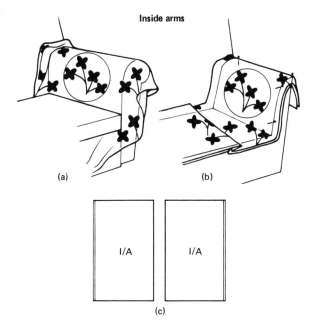

Inside arms

(a)   (b)

(c)

Figure 42

The starting point for cutting the centred width will be 1 in (2.5 cm) *above* the mark. Measure the length entered in column 3 of your list and cut as shown (in Figure 29e and f).

Matching a pattern on further widths

Identify the starting point of the centred width at the selvedge and cut each further width to match, as shown for I/Bs, Figure 31. Cut until you have the number of widths entered in column 4 of your list.

Cutting half-width inside arms

Cut at the centre fold (Figure 42c). Place a half-width on each arm.

Placing

Place both arms before proceeding to the next main piece. Pin the piece to the arm, centre-to-centre, and pin it at top and front, ensuring that there is enough for seams. Trim the allowance at the top as far as the inside back, and at the front (Figure 43a to p).

Arm with back only.   Turn up a hem before placing. If the arm
has a wooden top (Figure 43a) pin the piece to the upholstery,
allowing for seams beyond the wood at top and front; if it is
upholstered take the arm material round to the O/B, cutting and
snipping as shown in Figure 43d. Shape round a wing as shown
in Figure 43g to j.

Figure 43

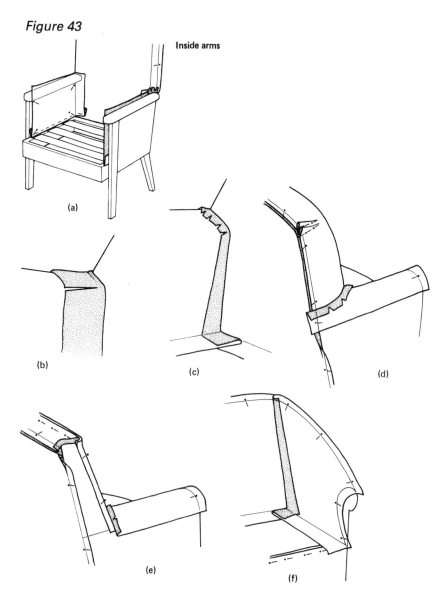

Inside arms

(a)

(b)

(c)

(d)

(e)

(f)

Trim the back of the arm from top to seat, allowing 1 in (2.5 cm) at the top, sharply increasing to the same amount of tuck-in as you've allowed on the inside back.

Arm shaped over curve at back.   Fold back the material and slash it parallel with the arm at the same place as on the inside back (Figure 43b). Trim from the curve to the seat, then cut and snip from the curve to the outside of the arm in the same way as for the inside back (Figure 43c). If the arm extends round the back cut and snip as shown in Figure 43d; if it finishes where it meets the back cut and snip as shown in Figure 43e.

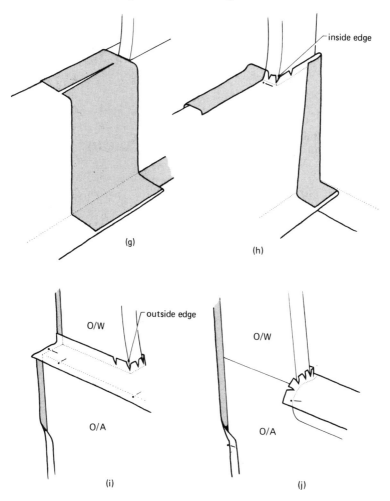

Sloping arm.   Trim the back of the arm from the top to the seat. Allow for the seam at the top, sharply increasing to as much as possible for tuck-in, up to the amount allowed on the inside back at this point (Figure 43f).

Arm shaped round a wing.   Fold back the material close against the front of the wing and slash it to within 1 in (2.5 cm) of the centre front. Slash parallel with the arm and do not pull the material away from the wing when cutting or you will cut too far (Figure 43g).

Pin the piece to the arm in front of the wing, then snip almost to the line of shaping at the inside edge of the wing.

Figure 43 (continued)

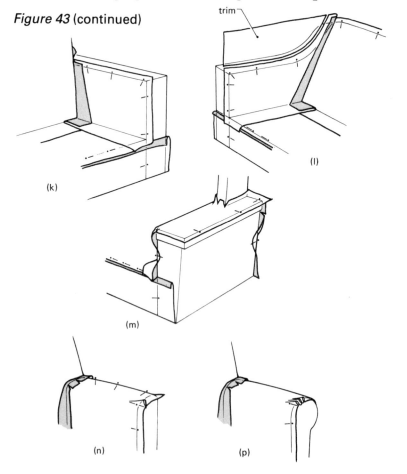

To find the exact place, snip a little less than necessary and adjust the material, then snip again. Take care not to cut too far as the line of shaping is the seam line. Cut and snip as far as the inside back then fold the material against the back and trim, allowing for the seam at the top and tuck-in at the side. Allow as much tuck-in as possible up to the amount allowed for the inside back at this point (Figure 43h).

If the arm extends round the back of the wing snip at the outside edge of the wing and cut, allowing for seam (Figure 43i); if the arm finishes at the wing cut and snip round the back of the arm, allowing for the seam (Figure 43j). Pin the back of the arm in place.

Arm with T/A or border. Trim, allowing for seams at T/A (Figure 43k and l) or border (Figure 43m) as shown. Shape the back of the arm, allowing for tuck-in as directed for a sloping arm (see above).

Arms with darts. Some arms require darts at the inside curve of the front to dispose of fullness. Fit as many darts as necessary, bearing in mind that two or three short, small darts are less noticeable than one long one (Figure 43n and p).

OUTSIDE ARMS

Centring a pattern
Find the starting point in the same way as for the outside back, page 64. Measure at the selvedge the length entered in column 3 of your list and cut.

Matching a pattern on further widths
Identify the starting point of the centred width at the selvedge and cut each further width to match as shown for I/Bs, (Figure 31). Cut until you have the number of widths entered in column 4 of your list.

Cutting half-width outside arms
As for inside arms. Follow the same procedure.

Placing

Place both arms before proceeding to the next main piece. Pin up
a hem if necessary. Pin the bottom of the piece to the bottom of
the arm, centre-to-centre, and to the top, centre-to-centre. Pin at
the sides and trim the allowances (Figure 44a to k).

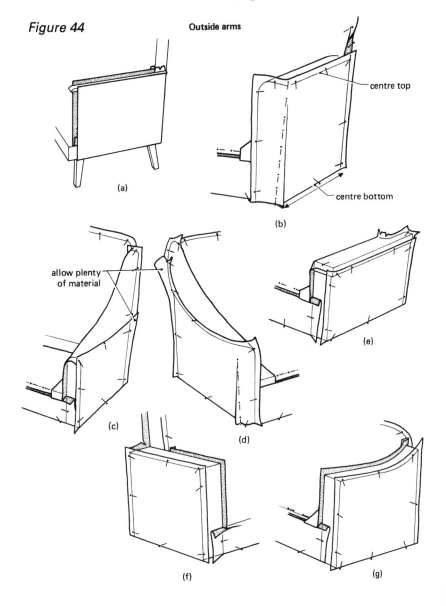

Figure 44   Outside arms

(a)

centre top

centre bottom

(b)

allow plenty
of material

(c)

(d)

(e)

(f)

(g)

Arm with wooden top. Allow beyond the wood for seams (Figure 44a).

Arm and front in one. Centre the piece on the outside only, but take the arm material to the front. Fit a dart at the outside edge of the front (Figure 44b).

Arm with curved or overhanging edge. Let the top of the piece stand away slightly from the underside of the edge. Allow more than the usual 1 in (2.5 cm) for seams where the arm joins the outside back at the top, as it is sometimes difficult to tell where the seam should be at this stage (Figure 44c, d and e).

Arm with border. Figure 44f and g shows how the arm material is placed and trimmed.

Roll arm. Pin directly under the roll each side (Figure 44h). To dispose of the droop in the middle, smooth the slack out to the top and adjust the pins. Trim off surplus material at the top, allowing for the seam (Figure 44i). The cover will stand away from the chair at the middle of the roll but will look quite acceptable.

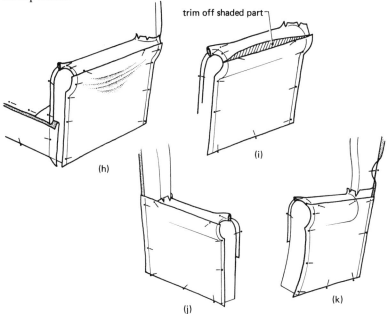

trim off shaded part

(h)

(i)

(j)

(k)

Another way of dealing with this problem is to disregard the droop while fitting and to fix the finished cover under the roll with upholstery pins, but this is not recommended. The pins screw in. Unfortunately they tend to unscrew quite easily, and the repeated replacing of the pins can damage the upholstery and frame.

Arm with wing.   Take the piece to the back of the chair whether the arm extends to the back or not (Figure 44j and k).

INSIDE AND OUTSIDE WINGS

Centring a pattern on the inside wings

Strictly speaking the pattern is not centred but matched to the inside back so that the same part continues across the chair, giving the illusion of back and wings in one (Figure 45). The left

Figure 45

wing is therefore cut from the left side of the material, and the right wing from the right side.

Fold and drape the material on the left wing with the selvedge close to the line of shaping where the wing is widest. Adjust until the pattern follows on from the I/B and pin in place. Stand back to judge the effect. When satisfied that the pattern is level mark with a pin the top of the wing where it is longest (Figure 46).

Take the material off the chair and open it out. Cut 1 in (2.5 cm) *above* the pin to allow for the seam. This is the starting point for cutting the 'centred' width. Measure at the selvedge the length entered in column 3 of your list and cut.

Figure 46

Matching a pattern on further widths for inside wings
Identify the starting point of the centred width at the selvedge
and cut each further width to match as shown in Figure 47,
choosing the appropriate width of wing. Cut until you have the
number of widths entered in column 4 of your list.

Matching a pattern on outside wings
Although outside wings do not have to match, when more than
one item is being covered it is worth trying to match all left-hand
and all right-hand wings as far as possible.

Cutting inside and outside wings in patterned material
Cut as shown in the appropriate Figures.

Quarter-width inside and outside wings. All wings as in Figure 47a.
Trim one pair per width to the correct length for the shorter
wings.

Quarter-width inside wings with half-width outside wings. I/Ws, Figure 47b. O/Ws, Figure 48c, same as for plain material.

Half-width inside wings with quarter-width outside wings. I/Ws, Figure 47c. O/Ws, Figure 48b, same as for plain material.

Half-width inside and outside wings. I/Ws, Figure 47c, O/Ws, Figure 48c, same as for plain material.

Figure 47

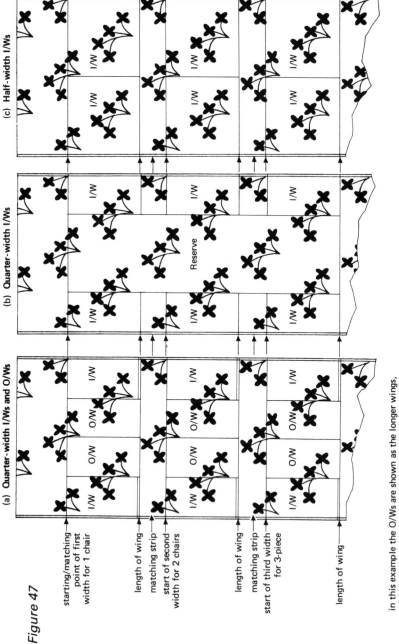

(a) Quarter-width I/Ws and O/Ws

(b) Quarter-width I/Ws

(c) Half-width I/Ws

starting/matching
point of first
width for 1 chair

length of wing
matching strip
start of second
width for 2 chairs

length of wing
matching strip
start of third width
for 3-piece

length of wing

In this example the O/Ws are shown as the longer wings,
with the I/Ws trimmed to their proper length.
As the reverse could well be the case, check that you are trimming the correct wings

Cutting inside and outside wings in plain material

Measure at the selvedge the length entered in column 3 of your list and cut. Cut as many widths as required in column 4. Cut the wings to the size as shown in appropriate diagrams:

Quarter-width inside and outside wings. All wings, Figure 48a. Trim one pair to the correct length for the shorter wing if covering one chair or a three-piece suit.

Quarter-width inside wings with half-width outside wings. I/Ws, Figure 48b; O/Ws, Figure 48c.

Figure 48

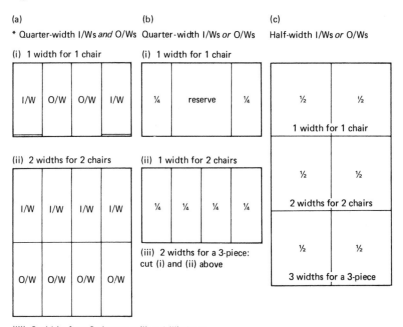

(a)

* Quarter-width I/Ws *and* O/Ws

(i) 1 width for 1 chair

| I/W | O/W | O/W | I/W |

(ii) 2 widths for 2 chairs

| I/W | I/W | I/W | I/W |

| O/W | O/W | O/W | O/W |

(iii) 3 widths for a 3-piece: cut (i) and (ii) above

(b)

Quarter-width I/Ws *or* O/Ws

(i) 1 width for 1 chair

| ¼ | reserve | ¼ |

(ii) 1 width for 2 chairs

| ¼ | ¼ | ¼ | ¼ |

(iii) 2 widths for a 3-piece: cut (i) and (ii) above

(c)

Half-width I/Ws *or* O/Ws

| ½ | ½ |

1 width for 1 chair

| ½ | ½ |

2 widths for 2 chairs

| ½ | ½ |

3 widths for a 3-piece

* Quarter-width I/Ws *and* O/Ws for 1 chair or a 3-piece :
In the example above the O/Ws are shown as the longer wings.
As the reverse could well be the case, check that you are trimming the correct wings

Half-width inside wings with quarter-width outside wings.   I/Ws, Figure 48c, O/Ws, Figure 48b.

Half-width inside and outside wings.   All wings, Figure 48c.

Placing

Place the left piece on the left wing and the right piece on the right wing. Pin up hems before placing wings over wooden arms.

Inside wing.   Place the I/W pieces so that they follow the main line of the I/B, rather than the individual shape of the wing. The I/Ws should look as if they are as one with the I/B, whether patterned or not. Allow 1 in (2.5 cm) for the seam where the wing is widest and longest (Figure 49a). Pin at top and front, taking the piece round the fullness of the wing to meet the outside wing at the same place as on the upholstery. Trim the allowances and pin short, small darts behind the fullness, so that they are not conspicuous from the front (Figure 49b). If the wing has a border take the piece as far as the border and trim, ensuring that there is enough for a seam all round (Figure 49c).

Figure 49

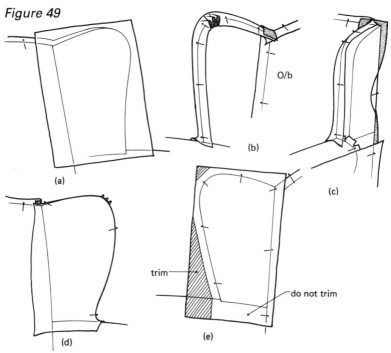

Trim the tuck-in to 1 in (2.5 cm) at the top where there is no recess. Trim the remainder of the tuck-in if necessary, to the depth of recess plus seam (Figure 49d).

Outside wing. Allow the exact 1 in (2.5 cm) for the seam all down the back to keep the wing straight with the main line of the outside back, and 1 in (2.5 cm) at the top where the wing is longest. Pin at top and sides and trim the allowances. Do not trim the allowance at the bottom (Figure 49e).

FRONT ARMS

Estimated front arms

Centring a pattern. The front arms will not be a matching pair if the pattern is centred in the usual way, because the opposite shaping would show the pattern differently (Figure 50a). Most

Figure 50

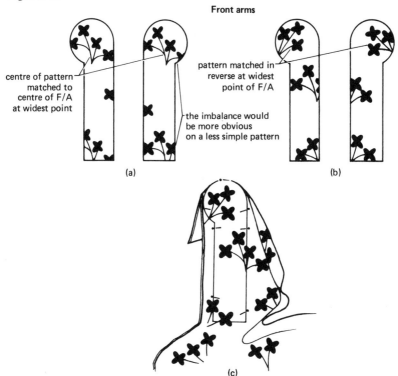

Front arms

centre of pattern matched to centre of F/A at widest point

pattern matched in reverse at widest point of F/A

the imbalance would be more obvious on a less simple pattern

(a)   (b)

(c)

patterns are well balanced, however. If there is a spray of flowers at one selvedge there will be a similar spray in reverse on the same level at the other selvedge. This enables the front arms to be paired in reverse by cutting the left front arm from the left side of the material, and the right front arm from the right side (Figure 50b). Although the front arms do not match exactly, they look better than if they showed quite different parts of the pattern.

Pin the material against the left front arm so that an attractive part of the pattern shows on the wide part. Allow for a seam at the outside where the arm is widest. Mark the top with a pin where the front arm is longest (Figure 50c).

Take the material off the arm and cut 1 in (2.5 cm) *above* the mark to allow for the seam. This is the starting point for cutting the width. Measure at the left selvedge the length entered in column 3 of your list and cut.

Matching a pattern on further widths. Identify the starting point of the first width at the selvedge and cut each further width to match, until you have the number of widths estimated in column 4 of your list.

Quarter-width front arms. Cut and match patterned quarter widths in the same way as for wings, Figure 47b. Cut plain quarter widths as shown in Figure 51.

Quarter-width F/As in plain material

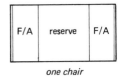

one chair

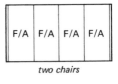

two chairs

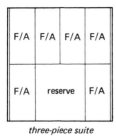

three-piece suite

Figure 51

Half-width front arms. Cut in the same way as for wings: patterned half widths as shown in Figure 47c, plain half widths as shown in Figure 48c.

Placing

Pin up hems if necessary. Place the left piece on the left front arm and the right piece on the right front arm. Pin from the bottom

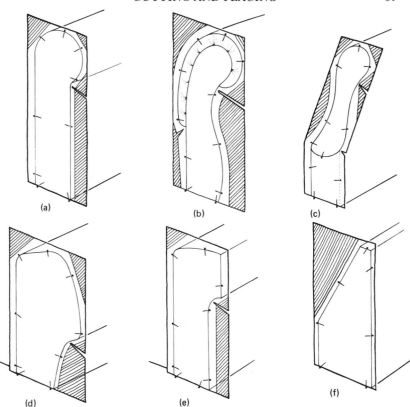

(a)

(b)

(c)

(d)

(e)

(f)

Figure 52

up, keeping the piece straight. Pin to the arm at the sides. Slash diagonally into the corners and trim the allowance (Figure 52).

Front arms from trimmings

Find a pair of trimmings for each item to be covered as directed in Minor Pieces, page 84. Cut the trimmings to size, allowing for seams and a hem if necessary.

Place as directed above.

TOP ARMS

Estimated from the length of the material

Centring a pattern and matching further widths. The left- and right-hand pieces can be paired by cutting from the middle of each half

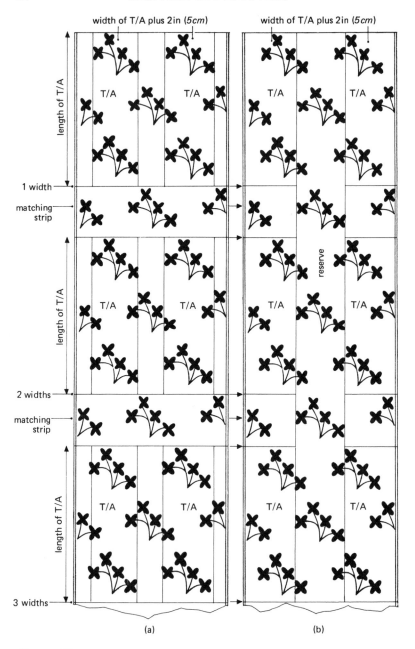

Figure 53

width (Figure 53a) or paired in reverse by cutting at each selvedge (Figure 53b). Both look well, but the second is more economical as the one strip left over will be more useful for other parts of the cover – for frill especially, if it is wide enough.

It is not necessary to find a particular starting point in order to centre the pattern. Measure at the selvedge the length required in column 3 of your list and cut. If further widths are required they will have to be matched to the first width, however. Identify the starting point of the first width and cut each further width as shown in Figure 53.

Placing. Pin up a hem if necessary. Pin the piece to the arm from the bottom up to the top of the front, then to the back of the arm, ensuring that there is enough for a seam all round (Figure 54a).

Estimated from the width of the material

Measure at the selvedge the length entered in column 3 of your list and cut the number of widths required in column 4.

Placing

Top arm up to 48 in (122 cm). Pin up a hem if necessary. Pin the piece to the arm in the same way as for top arms estimated from the length of the material (Figure 54a).

Top arm more than 48 in (122 cm). Pin a width to the top of the arm and trim to size, allowing for seams at back and front. From a width cut a piece the length of the front plus allowance for a

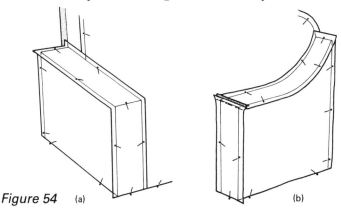

Figure 54 (a)   (b)

seam and also a hem if necessary. Pin up a hem. Pin the piece to the front from the bottom up, ensuring that there is enough for seams each side. Pin the pieces together at the top of the front (Figure 54b).

MINOR PIECES

Cutting

Patterned small shapes.   Look for a pair of trimmings off the sides of a symmetrical main piece, as the pair will match in reverse (Figure 55). (See centring a pattern, page 79 for an explanation of matching in reverse.) If covering more than one item of the same style you will find matching pairs from the same places on the other items.

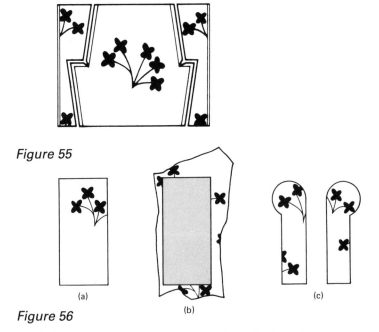

Figure 55

(a)   (b)   (c)

Figure 56

If there are no matching trimmings find a piece with a large splurge of pattern that will fill up the widest part of the shape. Cut the trimming to size, allowing for seams and a hem if necessary (Figure 56a), then lay it face down on another trimming with a similar splurge and cut the second piece to size from the first (Figure 56b). The pair will give the illusion of matching (Figure 56c).

Plain small shapes.   If possible use trimmings from the length of the material.

Borders, plain or patterned.   Use trimmings if available, or cut strips from the width of the material. Allow for seams and a hem if necessary.

Placing

Small shapes.   Place minor front arms the same as you would estimated ones, (page 80). All small shapes should be filled in as soon as suitable trimmings become available, following the joins in the upholstery as to shape.

Borders.   Pin up hems if necessary before placing. Pin a vertical border from the bottom up, and a horizontal border from front to back. Check continually that there is enough for seams all along the sides (Figure 57a to k).

Side borders to fireside chair back.   Snip almost to the line of shaping under front rolls (Figure 57b) or back rolls (Figure 57c). Pin hems above and below wooden arms before placing borders (Figure 57d).

Side borders to armchair back.   Allow the exact 1 in (2.5 cm) for the seam at the back to keep the borders straight. Trim the allowances (Figure 57e).

Side borders to seat.   If the back of the chair does not have side borders, the seat borders should extend all the way to the outside back (Figure 57f); otherwise take the pieces as far as the side borders of the back and trim, allowing for a seam (Figure 57g).

Border below seat.   Cut the width to size for the front, allowing for narrow hems at the sides. Pin the piece on the front and pin darts at the sides of the top. Pin to the underseat. If there are borders at the sides cut a width into two pieces and pin it to the borders, allowing for a seam at the back and a narrow hem at the front.

Pin to the underseat (Figure 57h). Side borders should extend as far back as shown in Figure 57f or 57g, as appropriate.

Borders on arms.   If the tops of the arms are wooden, pin narrow hems at the top of the front borders. Shape the top borders over the back of the arm in the same way as for the inside back (Figure 57j). If the arms have wooden tips, place borders on the fronts, as on the fronts shown on Figure 57j.

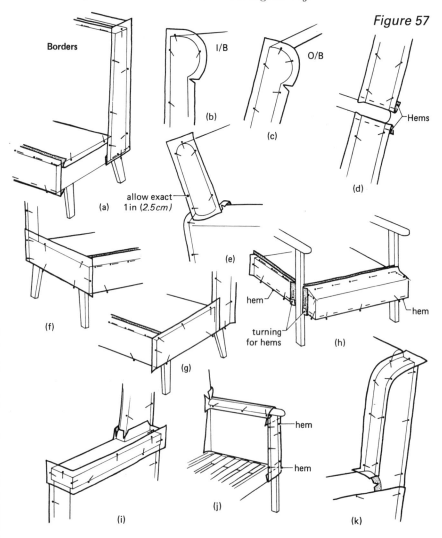

Figure 57

Borders on wings.   Place as shown in Figure 57k, allowing for seams at top and bottom.

TRIMMINGS

Now is the time to sort out the useful trimmings and throw away those that are not. Sort into separate bags as follows and label:

Frill

Strips from the length or width of the material. Trim to the length of the frill plus 2 in (5 cm) allowances.

Skirt

Strips from the width of the material. Trim to the length of the skirt plus 2 in (5 cm) allowances.

Borders for boxed cushions

Strips from the width of the material. Trim to the length of the border plus 1¼ in (3 cm) for seams. Strips cut out when matching a patterned material should be earmarked for front borders, as the strips themselves will match.

Openings for boxed cushions

Strips from the width or length of the material, at least half the length of the border plus seams. Two strips are required per opening, but save as many as possible. They will be trimmed to the correct width when the openings are assembled.

Flaps for plain-tailored covers

Four pieces 12 × 6 in (30 × 15 cm) are required per chair; two pieces 12 × 6 in (30 × 15 cm) and two pieces 24 × 6 in (61 × 15 cm) are needed for a settee.

Facings

Save a few bias strips and straight strips, 2–3 in (5–7.5 cm) wide, in case they are needed for facings.

Piping

Trim suitable pieces to rough squares or oblongs.

CUSHION COVERS

If the cushion covers are to go with the chair/settee covers cut all the pieces for the cushions before continuing with the fitting of the larger items, so that if a little more material is needed it is more likely to be in stock.

If making cushion covers only, read the general directions in the introduction to this section, many of which apply to cushions.

See Figure 58 for the various parts of a boxed cushion and their positions.

Tops and bottoms

Measure and cut the length required in column 3 of your list for as many widths as required in column 4.

Centring and matching a pattern. Find the starting point before measuring the length required, by measuring up from the centre

Figure 58

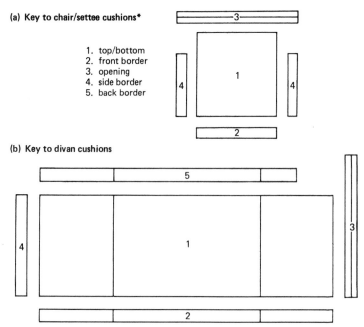

(a) **Key to chair/settee cushions***

1. top/bottom
2. front border
3. opening
4. side border
5. back border

(b) **Key to divan cushions**

stand-up chair/sette cushions: pieces 2 and 3 are reversed so that the opening is concealed at the bottom of the cushion

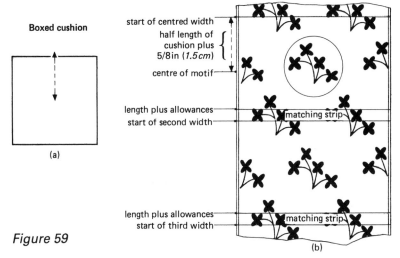

Boxed cushion

(a)

start of centred width
half length of
cushion plus
5/8in (1.5cm)
centre of motif

length plus allowances
start of second width

matching strip

length plus allowances
start of third width

matching strip

(b)

Figure 59

of the main motif half the actual length of the cushion at its longest point, plus ⅝ in (1.5 cm) for the seam.

Figure 59b shows the middle motif centred for a full-width piece. When half widths are required the motifs at the sides are centred as in Figure 4b, but the method is the same.

If more than one width is required in column 4 of your list find the starting point for each width before measuring and cutting. Again, the method is the same for one-width pieces as in Figure 59b, and for half-width pieces as shown in Figure 47c, for inside wings.

Figure 60

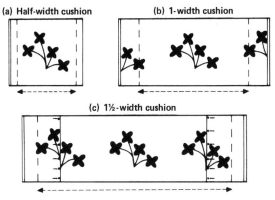

(a) Half-width cushion   (b) 1-width cushion

(c) 1½-width cushion

◀------▶ width of cushion at widest point plus 1¼ in (3cm) for seams

Cutting and assembling widths. Cut half-width pieces at the centre fold. Cut and assemble one-and-a-half-width and two-width pieces, as for inside backs, pages 56–7.

Trim each piece to the width of the cushion at its widest point plus 1¼ in (3 cm) for seams. Trim equally at the sides to keep a pattern motif central and part widths even (Figure 60).

Fitting. Do not fit the pieces on the cushion unless the shape is very complicated or the cushion is too floppy to be made from measurements (Figure 25d and l).

If the cushion has to be fitted, label and mark the pieces which are to be put aside for later fitting as soon as they are cut; place pieces for immediate fitting on the cushion as soon as they are cut, and fit as directed on page 106.

Shaping from measurements. This is much easier than fitting, and the covers look better because they hide misshapen parts of the cushion which fitted covers are more likely to duplicate.

Draw the shape with tailor's chalk on the wrong side of one of the pieces, ensuring that a pattern or texture is running the right way; i.e. from the back to the front of the cushion (top to bottom of a stand-up cushion).

If the cushion narrows at the back and the shaping is all on one side, mark the difference in width at the back on that side, but if the shaping is symmetrical mark half the difference. Draw a seam line to the mark (Figure 61a). Mark the dimensions of an angular shape and draw a seam line to join up the marks (Figure 61b). To reproduce a rounded shape pin the piece wrong side out on the cushion, allowing for seams all round, and rub tailor's chalk over the shaped part (Figure 61c).

Cut ⅝ in (1.5 cm) outside the shaping (Figure 61d). If the shape is symmetrical pin the piece in half lengthways and use the first side as a guide for cutting the second side (Figure 61e); if differently shaped, mark and trim the second side in the same way as the first.

When one piece is fully shaped it can be used as a pattern for any number of alike pieces. Lay the pieces wrong sides together with the 'pattern' piece on top, pin and cut (Figure 61f). Tops and bottoms for reversed shapes (Figure 61g) can be cut from the same pattern piece as follows: cut two pieces to shape with the pattern and piece wrong sides together, then one with the right side of the pattern to the wrong side of the piece.

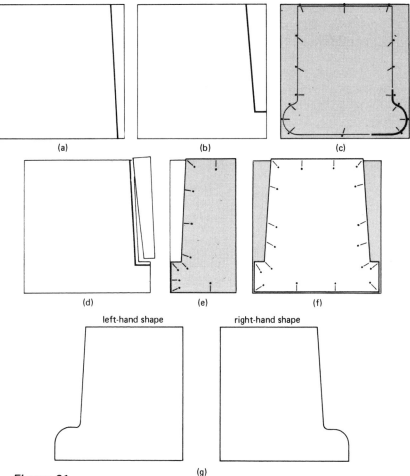

(a)   (b)   (c)

(d)   (e)   (f)

left-hand shape   right-hand shape

(g)

Figure 61

Label and mark tops and bottoms as soon as they are shaped, and put aside until all pieces are ready for sewing.

Borders

Openings. Use widthways or lengthways strips from trimmings as far as possible. When these run out, or if none are available, cut strips from the width of the material as required.

The opening must be wide enough for the cover to go on and off the cushion without strain: about 7–8 in (17–20 cm) wider than the back of a fairly square chair/settee cushion, or the side of a divan cushion. To accommodate a T-shaped cushion, however, the opening would have to extend almost all the way down the sides.

The width of the opening will also depend to some extent on whether the cushion is rigid or can be squashed (a little) into the cover. Allow a little more than you think necessary when deciding upon the width of the opening.

Cut two pieces per opening, each half the length of the border plus: 1¼ in (3 cm) for a zip fastener, 2 in (5 cm) for hook and eyelet tape or 3 in (7.5 cm) for hand-sewn hooks and eyes.

Figure 62

Pin the pieces together with the top overlapping on the outside, so that combined they come to the length of the border plus ⅝ in (1.5 cm) for seams at top and bottom (Figure 62). If hooks and eyes are to be sewn by hand the necessary allowances will get in the way, so pin 1 in (2.5 cm) hems with ⅜ in (1 cm) turned in at the bottom of the upper piece and at the top of the lower piece before overlapping (Figure 63).

Figure 63

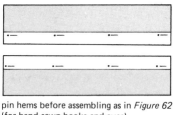

pin hems before assembling as in *Figure 62*
(for hand-sewn hooks and eyes)

Put the openings aside for sewing.

Front borders.   Cut the number of widths required, less any that you have put aside from trimmings, bearing in mind that all front borders should match whether obtained from trimmings, cut as estimated, or some of each. Cut the trimmings/widths to the length required in column 3 of your list.

You will require:

half-width pieces: one width per pair of cushions, cut into half widths.

one-width pieces: one width per cushion.

one-and-a-half- or two-width pieces: two widths per cushion.

Assemble one-and-a-half- or two-width front borders the same as for tops and bottoms.

Trim borders to the width of the cushion at its widest point, plus seam allowance, the same as for tops and bottoms, label and put aside for sewing.

Side borders. Cut from trimmings or from the width of the material as required, to the length entered in column 3 of your list.

On chair/settee cushions the width of the side border will depend on how far the opening extends round each side, but one width cut into half widths should be enough for two sides. For divan cushions cut one width per cushion and trim to the required width plus 1¼ in (3 cm) for seams.

Label side borders and put them aside for sewing.

Back borders for divan cushions. Cut and assemble these the same as for front borders. The width of the back border will depend on how far the opening extends round the back, but this can be adjusted when the cover is being sewn. Label these and put them aside for sewing.

Cushion covers only

If making cushion covers only, turn to page 138 for directions on sewing.

4

FITTING

CHAIR/SETTEE COVERS

When nothing remains to be seen of the chair the pieces can be pinned to each other and released from the chair. Use lots of pins, especially round curves or elaborate shapes, where pins should be head to tail. And keep them in line – never forget that the lines of pins are going to be your seam lines.

Pin firmly without pulling at the pieces. The term loose as applied to covers means that they can be removed and put on again, not that they should hang about the chair dejectedly. Covers should *fit* – not too loosely, not too tightly.

Follow the contours of the chair, feeling the joins in the upholstery with your fingertips as you pin to reproduce a good shape. Where there are no joins, across the outside of a roll arm, for instance, take special care to keep the line true.

The order given for pinning the seams is as consistent as possible with the order in which the seams are prepared and sewn up. Stick to it to retain a good, crisp shape.

FIRESIDE/TV CHAIRS

Pin as appropriate:

Backs
Basic.   I/B to O/B all round (Figure 64a).

With side borders.   I/B to borders. O/B to borders and top of I/B (Figure 64b).

Fireside/TV backs

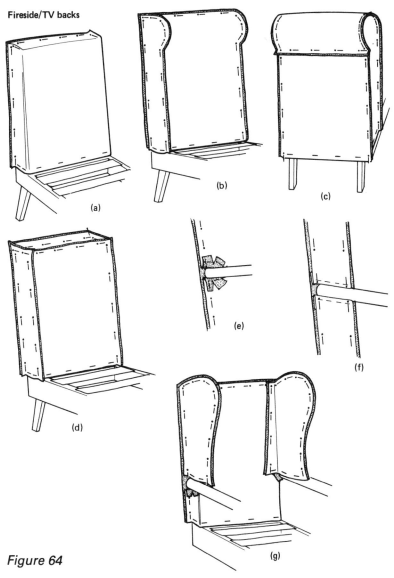

Figure 64

With side borders and outside roll. I/B to borders. O/B to borders. O/B to I/B below roll. If the middle of the O/B droops take up a little more in the seam allowance. It does not matter if this part stands away from the chair slightly (Figure 64c).

With top and side borders. Side borders to top border. I/B to borders. O/B to borders (Figure 64d).

With wooden arms. Pin the ends of seams as close to the arms as possible (Figure 64e or f).

With wings over wooden arms. I/Ws to O/Ws as shown in Figure 69. I/B to I/Ws. O/B to O/W and I/B each side. I/B to O/B at top (Figure 64g).

The above types of covers may now be taken off the chair and prepared for sewing. See Making an Opening and Removing the Cover, page 105.

Backs and seats

Pin the back as applicable above.

Basic. Release the seat border and fold it level with the tuck-in. Without disturbing the position of the material, shape down the tuck-in and to go across to the O/B, allowing for the seam. Snip carefully almost to the seam line into the corner of the border where it will meet the bottom of the tuck-in (Figure 65a). Pin the seat border to the tuck-in and across to the O/B. Pin the O/B to the seat border (Figure 65b). Shape and pin the other side in the same way.

If the seat has a front border pin the side borders to the front border (Figure 65c). Pin the borders to the seat (Figure 65c or d).

I/B with side borders. Carefully snip the bottom of the tuck-in almost to the seam line. Pin the I/B and seat to their respective borders, down to the bottom of the tuck-in (Figure 65e). Pin the borders together below the tuck-in (Figure 65f).

Complete the remainder of the seat seam(s) as shown in Figure 65c or d.

Upholstered borders below seat

If there are side borders below the seat, complete the seams at the back of the chair as shown in Figure 65a and b or e and f.

Figure 65

Fireside/TV backs and seats

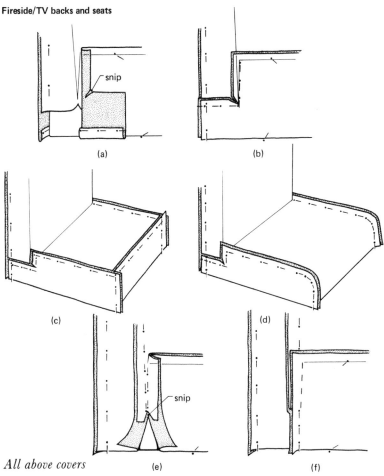

(a)

(b)

(c)

(d)

All above covers

(e)

(f)

The above types of covers may now be taken off the chair and prepared for sewing. See Making an Opening and Removing the Cover, page 105.

BACKS WITH ARMS AND WINGS

This type (see Figure 37j) can be treated as an armchair, the only difference being that the cover will not have a seat. Pin the seams in the same way as for an armchair, disregarding references to seat and seat front.

ARMCHAIRS

Tuck-in seams

Back shaped over arms. If the back has side borders first pin several inches of the I/B-to-border seams where they meet the arms (Figure 66a or c). If the arms have inside seams which finish at the I/B first pin several inches at this point (Figure 66b or c). Pin tuck-in seams from the back of the chair to the seat (as shown fully in Figure 66d and e).

Back with sloping arms. Pin tuck-in seams from the top of the I/B to the seat (Figure 66f).

Back with wings. Pin several inches of the I/W-to-I/A seams where they meet the I/B tuck-in seams. Pin I/B tuck-in seams from the top to the seat (Figure 66g).

Sides of seat. Pin tuck-in seams at the sides of the seat. Try the tuck-in inside the seat to check that the seams do not pull the pieces out of shape, and adjust if necessary (Figure 66h).

Back of seat. Shape the corners of the tuck-in as follows: if the I/B is too long for the I/As fold the surplus material and pin (Figure 66i). If the I/As are too long for the I/B take them in at the seams leading to the corners and trim (Figure 66j). Since the corners are not seen, they do not have to be perfectly shaped.

On some chairs the frames obstruct these corners. To shape round the obstructions tuck the material inside the seat all round, snip carefully where the corners are bunched up and trim. Keep snipping and trimming a little at a time until the corners tuck away smoothly. Pin over the obstructions, pull out the tuck-in, and extend the shaping to meet up with the seams.

Seat with separate front. Push the tuck-in inside the seat. If there is too much for the recesses at the front taper the ends of the seams so that they almost reach the bottom (Figure 66k). Pin back any material that will get in the way and shape the sides of the front as follows: if the front is flush with the arms snip the side almost to the seam line and extend the front-to-seat seam to the bottom of the tuck-in (Figure 66l); if the front protrudes at the top snip almost to the seam line at the side and slash

Figure 66

Tuck-in seams

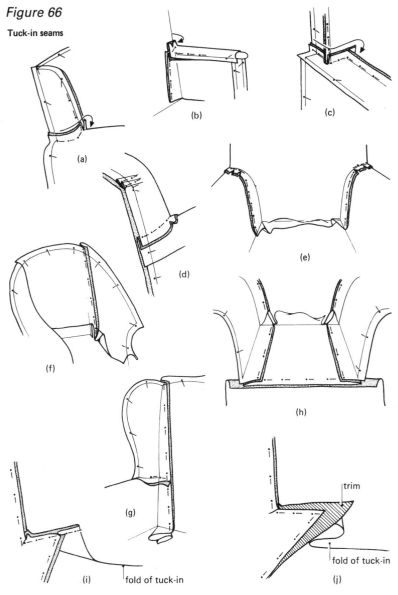

(a)

(b)

(c)

(d)

(e)

(f)

(g)

(h)

(i)   fold of tuck-in

(j)   trim   fold of tuck-in

diagonally into the corner where the front meets the arm, allowing ⅛ in (3mm) for the seam (Figure 66m). Trim, allowing for the seam. Extend the front-to-seat seam to the corner, and from the corner to the bottom of the tuck-in (Figure 66n).

Figure 66 (continued)

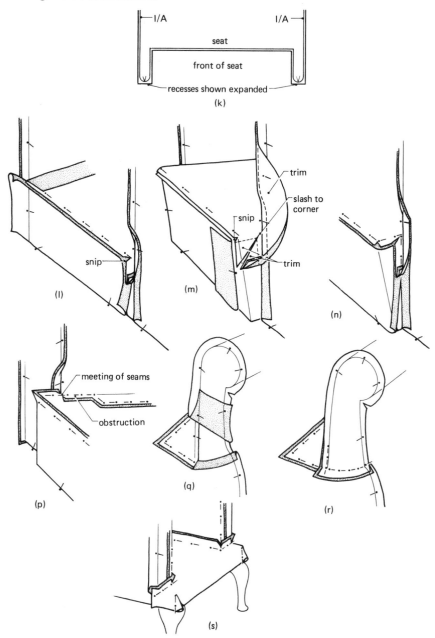

Note that when pinning from top to bottom of the tuck-in the seam must be pinned as far back as possible, flush with the arm, even though it will be difficult to get one's fingers into the cavities to do this.

If the frame obstructs the front of the seat, shape the tuck-in over the obstruction and pin the front-to-seat seam to meet up with the tuck-in-seam (Figure 66p).

Seat and front in one.   Pin the F/A out of the way and taper the front of the tuck-in seam to meet the inside of the arm. Pin as far as the arm (Figure 66q). Replace the F/A and pin several inches of the F/A-to-I/A seam. Continue the tuck-in seam round the bottom of the arm (Figure 66r). If the seat does not have a tuck-in pin several inches of the I/A-to-F/A seam, then pin the seat-to-I/A seam to extend round the bottom of the arm. Trim (Figure 66s).

Arm seams

Where there is a seat tuck-in the inside seam of the arm is pinned in two directions: from the bottom of the tuck-in up, as shown in Figure 67b; and from below the tuck-in down, as shown in Figure 67c. If there is no tuck-in pin the inside arm seam from the bottom of the chair up.

With roll.   O/A to I/A (Figure 67a). I/A and O/A to F/A (Figure 67b). Front to F/A (Figure 67c).

With roll and wing.   First pin several inches of the I/W-to-O/W seam. O/A to I/A and O/W (Figure 67d). Pin the front as shown in Figure 67b and c.

With roll as far as wing.   First pin several inches of the O/W-to-I/A seam. O/A to I/A and O/W (Figure 67e). Keep the seam straight, if necessary joining the O/W and O/A at a lower point than on the upholstery. It does not matter if the cover stands away from the chair slightly where the roll finishes. Pin the front as shown in Figure 67b and c.

With top arm.   O/A to T/A (Figure 67f or g). I/A to T/A from the bottom of the tuck-in up to the border of the I/B (Figure 67f) or to the top (Figure 67g). Front to T/A (Figure 67f or g).

Arm seams

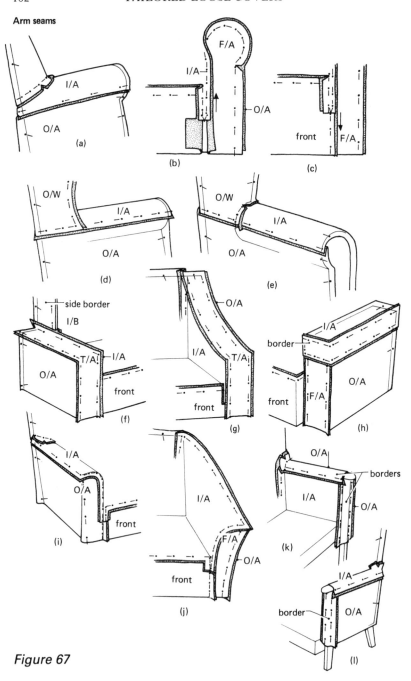

Figure 67

With border.   O/A to F/A. F/A and O/A to border. I/A to F/A and border. Front to F/A (Figure 67h).

Straight.   O/A to I/A. Front to O/A (Figure 67i).

Sloping.   O/A to I/A. I/A and O/A to F/A. Front to F/A (Figure 67j).

With wooden tops.   Front border to O/A and I/A. Top border to O/A and I/A (Figure 67k).

Wooden tips.   O/A to I/A. Front border to O/A and I/A (Figure 67l).

I/B side border seams
Complete I/B-to-side border seams (Figure 68a or b).

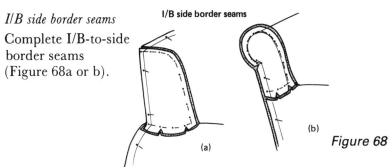

I/B side border seams

(a)

(b)

Figure 68

Wing Seams
Pin I/W to O/W. Complete the seams below the I/Ws as appropriate: to finish at the wing, in which case the I/W-to-O/W and I/W-to-I/A seams should finish up side by side (Figure 69a); or extend to the back of the chair (Figure 69b).

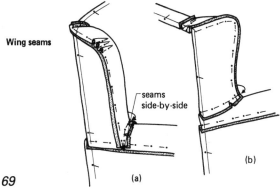

Wing seams

seams side-by-side

(b)

Figure 69

(a)

Back seams

Basic.   Pin the O/B to the rest of the cover (Figure 70a or b).

With outside roll.   O/B to O/A and border each side. O/B to I/B below roll (Figure 70c).

With wings.   O/B to O/W and O/A each side. O/B to I/B and I/Ws at top (Figure 70d or e); O/B to T/As (Figure 70e).

Back seams

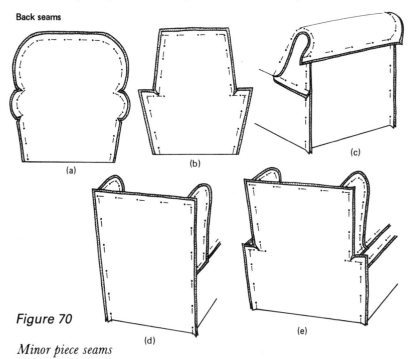

(a)   (b)   (c)

Figure 70

(d)   (e)

Minor piece seams

When all the main pieces are pinned together pin minor piece seams, if any, following the lines of the chair.

MEASURING FOR FRILL OR SKIRT

Make sure that the legs of the chair are on their correct levels, not for instance all four on a carpet when they are normally two on and two off.

Measure from the floor the finished length of the frill/skirt and mark with a pin, catching the material twice to secure. Tailor's chalk is not precise enough for this kind of marking. Measure at frequent intervals all round the chair. If the finished length is the recommended 6 in (15 cm), the measuring will be easier and more accurate if a 6 in (15 cm) rule is used (Figure 71).

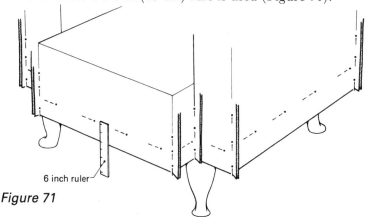

6 inch ruler

Figure 71

MAKING AN OPENING AND REMOVING THE COVER

First check that there are no bits of seams, darts, hems or turnings left unpinned. Also check that all the pins holding the material to the chair have been removed. Pull out any tuck-in that is inside the chair.

If the back of the chair is more or less the same width at top and bottom the cover may not need an opening. Lift the cover gently, a little at a time at back and front. If there is the slightest strain make an opening.

The opening should be at the O/B-to-O/A seam on the least noticeable side of an armchair/settee (Figure 72a). Part the seam

Figure 72

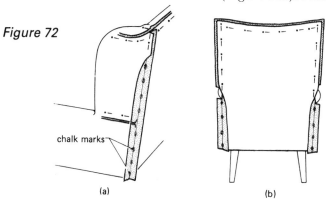

chalk marks

(a)   (b)

and rub tailor's chalk over the pins for about 12–18 in (30–45 cm) depending on how much wider at the top the back is, but if it is a lot wider mark the whole seam.

Open the seam for, say, 6 in (15 cm) and lift the cover gently, a little at a time at back and front. If there is any strain take out a few more pins, and so on until the cover lifts off easily.

When more than one item of furniture is being covered each should have the seam on its 'blind' side marked with chalk and opened.

Fireside chair with wooden arms

Two openings will be required, one below each arm as shown in Figure 72b. Also, if the back of the chair widens at the top one of the openings may have to extend above the arm in order to lift the cover off without strain. Mark seams with tailor's chalk and open as described above.

Fastenings

Measure the length of the opening and estimate for the type of fastening required (see Extras, page 47). Openings on alike items will vary slightly, so estimate the longest per chair/settee.

CUSHIONS

Pin the top and bottom right-sides-out and centre-to-centre on the cushion, ensuring that the material is running the right way and there is enough for seams all round. Trim roughly to shape leaving more than enough for seams and snip into corners almost to the seam line (Figure 73a).

Boxed cushions

Pin the border pieces to the cushion in the same way, referring to Figure 58 for the proper positions. Do not trim the width of the opening or side borders as yet (Figure 73b). Pin the border seams, then pin the border to the top and bottom (Figure 73c).

Take out the pins holding the material to the cushion and at the centre of the opening, and ease the cover off gently. If there is any strain adjust the opening-to-side border seams to give a wider opening.

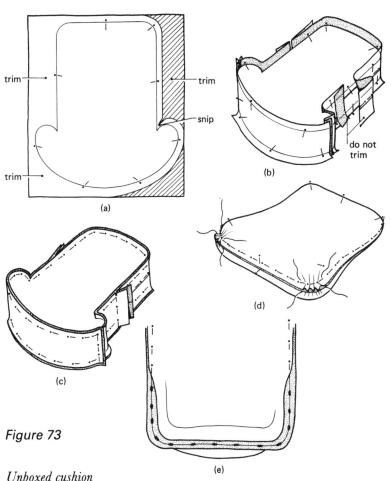

Figure 73

Unboxed cushion

Gather the top and bottom with needle and thread at the same places as on the cushion, then pin the top to the bottom all round (Figure 73d). Part the seam and rub tailor's chalk over the pins at the back, and for several inches on each side (Figure 73e). Take out the pins where marked and ease the cover off, marking and removing more pins each side if there is any strain.

Fastenings

Now that the width of the opening has been established, measure and estimate for the type of fastening required (see Extras, page 47).

5
PREPARING THE COVER FOR SEWING

TACKING

Professional covermakers do not usually tack covers but you are
strongly advised to do so. A workroom apprentice has experienced colleagues to guide her in the right direction when she
loses her way amongst the many seams of a cover. You must rely
on your tacking.

Use a different colour of cotton for darts and turnings and for
each seam or pair of seams. In the figures that follow each
different type of line represents a particular colour:

orange	·························	red	------------------
blue	▬▬▬▬▬	purple	—————··—··—
brown	— — — — —	yellow	------------------
green	—·—·—··—··—		

If you tack in these colours you will have no trouble finding
the parts of the cover you require at the preparing and sewing
stages, which have to be worked in a particular order.

Chair/settee covers

Lay the cover on its chair in a partly-on position so that you can
tell where the front, back and sides are; handle it gently while
looking for the parts you want or pins will fall out and the seams
will fray away.

Tack on the line of pins in the order given, using regular
stitches of about ½ in (1.25 cm). Secure each line firmly at the
start and finish; where a seam crosses the one you are tacking
leave a 1 in (2.5 cm) gap, finishing and starting again securely.

Do not tack joins (or disturb the pins) in one-and-a-half- and
two-width pieces for settee backs and seats.

Fireside/TV chairs

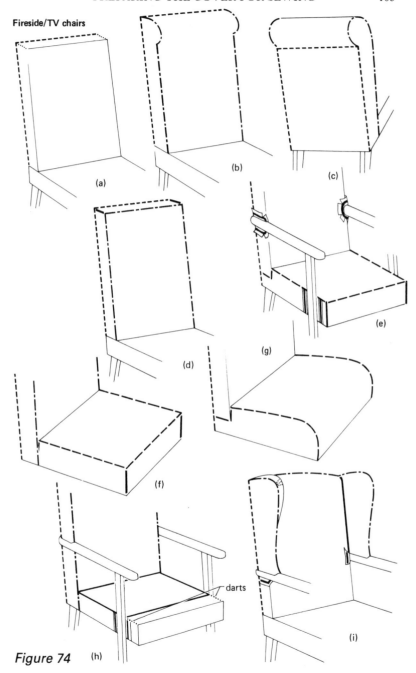

Figure 74

Cushion covers

Tack as described above in the same order in which you pinned. There is no need to identify the seams with differently coloured cottons. Do not tack joins (or disturb the pins) in one-and-a-half- and two-width pieces for divan cushions.

Fireside chairs/settees and TV chairs

Tack as appropriate, in the following order:

Orange (...........................) darts.   At I/B, seat, wings, etc. (Figure 74a, h and i).

Blue (———————) turnings and unpiped seams.   Turnings at arms and/or legs (Figure 74e, h and i).

   Seams joining borders together, at back or seat (Figure 74d, e and f).

   Underseat seams (Figure 74h).

   Tuck-in seams (Figure 74i).

Brown (—— —— —— ——) seat seams.   From arm to arm at front, and from arm to back each side (Figure 74e).

   One seam all round the seat (Figure 74f).

   From front to back each side (Figure 74g).

Green (—·——·——·——) I/B seams.   I/B-to-border seam each side (Figure 74b and c) on chairs without a top border; if with wooden arms: from top of arm to top of I/B each side, then from bottom of arm to bottom of I/B each side.

   I/B to border seam all round the back (Figure 74d) where the border is continuous; if with wooden arms: from top of arm on one side to the same place the other side, then from bottom of arm to bottom of I/B each side.

Red (-----------------) O/B seams (excepting openings).   Seam each side (Figure 74c and i).

   O/B-to-IB seam beneath a roll (Figure 74c).

   O/B seam all round (Figure 74a, b and d).

Green (—·——·——·——˙) I/B and wing seams.   From bottom of wing on one side to the same place on the opposite wing (Figure 74i).

Armchairs/settees

Tack as appropriate, in the following order:
Note: where the same seams occur on many styles only one or two examples are given in the text.

Orange (........................... *) darts.*   At I/B (Figure 75a and t); seat (Figure 75g and h); I/As (Figure 75b and c); O/As (Figure 75d and q); wings (Figure 75v).

Blue (——————————— *) unpiped seams*

Tuck-in seams from back of chair (Figure 75a) to seat (Figure 75b), and from front to back of seat (Figure 75b). Leave gaps at green seams of types shown in Figure 75m, w, x and y.

Seams below wings (Figure 75c) to extend to O/A (Figure 75k and l) or back of chair (Figure 75z). Leave gaps at green seams of types shown in Figure 75l and z.

Tuck-in seams from top of I/B to seat and from front to back of seat (Figure 75c and d).

Seat seams shaped over obstructions at front (Figure 75e) or with no tuck-in (Figure 75f), from front to back of seat.

Seats seams extending from outside of arm to seat, and from front to back of seat (Figure 75g and h). Leave gaps at yellow seams.

A further seat seam if I/B and seat are cut separately (Figure 75h).

Seams joining borders together (Figure 75x).

Seams at sides of protruding seat front (Figure 75p).

Brown (—— —— —— —— *) front seat seams.*   From bottom of tuck-in on one side to the same place the other side (Figure 75b); or if no tuck-in, from arm to arm (Figure 75e and f).

Seam under a rounded front, then side seams from under the roll to the bottom of the tuck-in (Figure 75i).

Purple (——--——--—— *)O/A seams.*   O/A seams from front to back (Figure 75j, k, l, m, n, p, s and t), with gaps at blue and green seams (Figure 75k) or blue seams (Figure 75l).

Yellow (------------------ *) I/A and F/A seams.*   F/A seams from bottom of F/A on outside to bottom of tuck-in, then from bottom of front to tuck-in (Figure 75b).

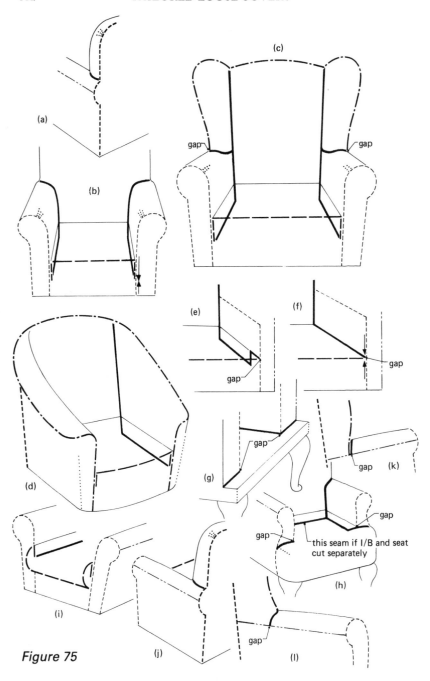

Figure 75

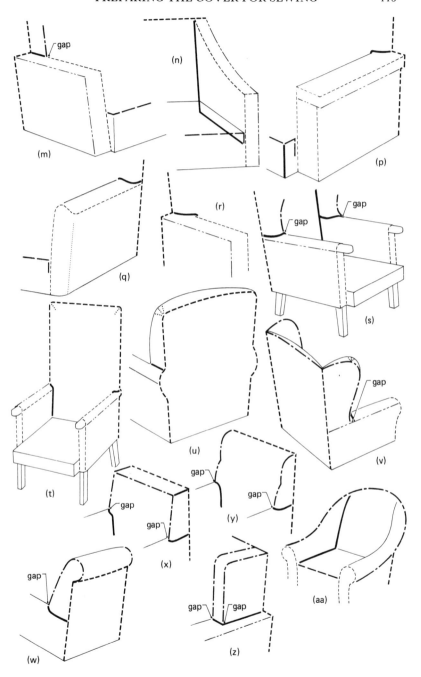

(m)

(n)

(p)

(q)

(r)

(s)

(t)

(u)

(v)

(w)

(x)

(y)

(z)

(aa)

gap

I/A seams from back of chair to bottom of tuck-in, then from bottom of front to tuck-in (Figure 75n, p and q); or from I/B to bottom of tuck-in, then from bottom of front to tuck-in (Figure 75m and r; see arrows on Figure 75b).

I/A seams as above, no tuck-in (Figure 75e and f): tack in the same directions to the front seat seam (see arrows, Figure 75f).

I/A seams from seat to back of chair, to finish as appropriate (Figure 75g).

F/A seams from seat to bottom of cover each side (Figure 75h). Leave gaps at blue seams and at darts.

Arm border seams at top on inside (Figure 75t); and at front from bottom of cover on outside to the same place on the inside (Figure 75s and t).

Extra seams at arms: top of F/A (Figure 75n), side of F/A (Figure 75p).

Green (—·——·——·—) *I/B seams.*   I/B-to-border seam each side (Figure 75w and y).

One seam all round the back (Figure 75x).

Red (-----------------) *O/B seam (excepting opening)*.   O/B seam all round (Figure 75t and u).

O/B seam each side (Figure 75d, v, w and aa).

O/B-to-I/B seam (Figure 75w).

Green (—·——·——·—) *back seams to be tacked after red seams.*   I/B and wing seam from bottom of wing on one side to the same place the other side (Figure 75c).

I/B and arm seam from bottom of front on one side to same place the other side (Figure 75d); or from F/A on one side to F/A on the other side (Figure 75aa).

Extra seams on wings with borders (Figure 75z).

TRIMMING AND NOTCHING

When all parts of the cover have been tacked it can be removed from the chair, and the rest of the preparation carried out in comfort.

Trim the allowances to ⅝ in (1.5 cm) *exactly*. At first measure ⅝ in (1.5 cm) from the tacking to the edges and mark with a biro to get your eye accustomed to the allowance. After one or two seams you will be able to trim to ⅝ in (1.5 cm) quite accurately without the tape measure.

Notch as you go, pinching the trimmed allowances and snipping at an angle. Keep the notches small, unevenly spaced and unevenly grouped (Figure 76).

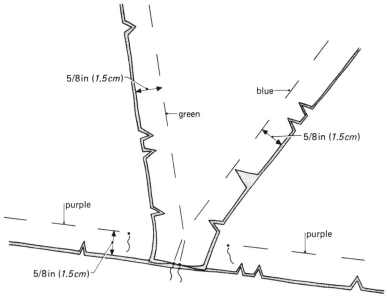

Figure 76

Trim and notch all seams and large darts, working in the same order as you tacked to keep the shape crisp.

Note that this is a precise operation which if not carried out properly will be the undoing of all the good work put into the fitting of the cover. Each seam has to be taken apart and turned to the inside for sewing. To retain the shape of the cover you must be able to put the pieces together again exactly as they were, by marrying up the notches; and you must know exactly where your seam lines are, i.e. ⅝ in (1.5 cm) from the edge of the material.

When covering more than one item trim and notch one cover at a time just before you intend to sew it, so that the material does not have time to fray in the interval between preparing and sewing.

MAKING UP PIPING

For an armchair/settee cover you will almost certainly require more piping than you can make out of trimmings, but if you use the trimmings up first you will find out how far a batch will go and will be better able to judge how much more you are likely to need.

Cutting bias strips
Make a marker out of cardboard, notched at 1½ in (4 cm).

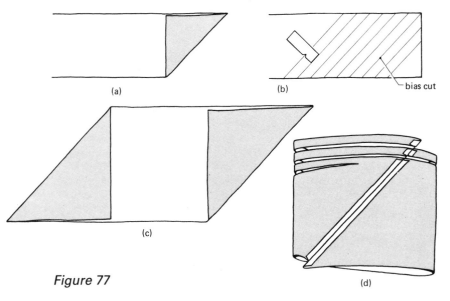

Figure 77

Strips from trimmings and other small pieces of material. Fold a corner of the piece on the bias and cut along the fold (Figure 77a). Cut 1½ in (4 cm)-wide strips parallel with the bias cut (Figure 77b).

Strips from a large piece of material. Fold the corners on the bias and cut (Figure 77c). Sew the bias edges right-sides-together, twisted so that one is 1½ in (4 cm) higher than the other. Cut a continuous 1½ in (4 cm)-wide strip (Figure 77d).

Joining bias strips
Join the strips right-sides-together and sew from angle to angle (Figure 78a). If sewn correctly the joins should have tails at top

Figure 78

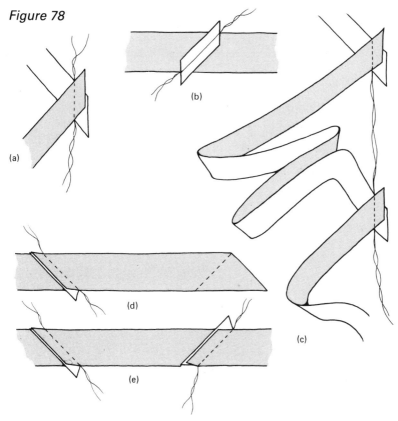

and bottom when opened out (Figure 78b). There is no need to cut the cotton after each join. Just release the pressure foot and pull out several inches of cotton before joining the next strip (Figure 78c). Put aside any strips that will not join because they are on the opposite bias. When all the strips are joined trim the last strip to the opposite bias (Figure 78d), and continue joining as before (Figure 78e).

Cut the loops of cotton between the joins.

Encasing the cord

Fold the casing over the cord, right-side-out and edges even. Using the piping/zipper foot, sew close to the cord without catching it in the stitching. Open out the joins in the casing as you go along. Do not cut the cord when all the casing is used, and leave the last strip partly unsewn.

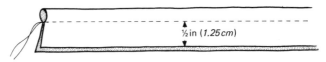

½ in (1.25 cm)

Figure 79

Trim the seam allowance to ½ in (1.25 cm) exactly (Figure 79). This is important as it is the piping that establishes the seam line in the piped seams. Also if the piping allowance was more than ½ in (1.25 cm) it would cover the notches on the bottom piece to be sewn, making it difficult to marry them up.

6

SEWING UP THE COVER

Sew as appropriate in the following order:

PINNED SEAMS ON ONE-AND-A-HALF- AND TWO-WIDTH SETTEE BACKS AND SEATS

Release the top piece (with the folded selvedge) from the pins, leaving the pins sticking out about half an inch (Figure 80a). Check that each pin is still at the very edge of the fold and that the selvedges are pinned together (Figure 80b). On the inside, sew where the top piece was folded; i.e. where the pins show a little on the selvedge line (Figure 80c). Sew slowly across the pins and you will not break the machine needle. Press the seam open.

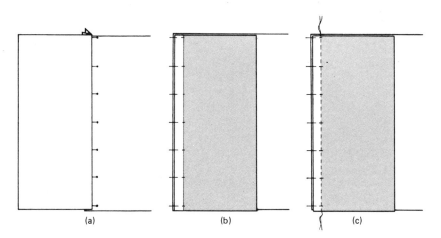

Figure 80

HEMS WITH FLAPS ON PLAIN-TAILORED COVERS

First shape and hem the flaps that are sewn into the hems (these will be used to fasten the cover in place – see Figure 100). Trim the flap to wedge shape, taking off 2 in (5 cm) at each side of the bottom, tapered to nothing at the top (Figure 81a). Sew narrow hems at the sides. At the bottom, sew a ¾ in (2 cm) slot with ¼ in (6 mm) turned in, back-stitching at the ends of the slot, which have to take a lot of strain (Figure 81b).

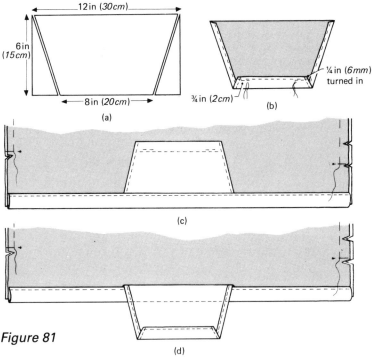

Figure 81

Undo the tacking of all seams at the hem and twist the loose ends of cotton round pins to secure them. At the front, place a flap centre-to-centre, wrong side of flap to wrong side of cover, with the unstitched edge ½ in (1.25 cm) inside the hem. Pin the flap in place and sew the hem (Figure 81c). Fold the flap down and sew it to the bottom edge of the cover (Figure 81d).

Insert flaps and sew hems at the back and sides in the same way, remembering that on a settee the wide flaps go at the back and front.

OTHER HEMS

Other hems can be sewn straightforwardly.

DARTS (orange)

Undo about 2 in (5 cm) of the seam each side of the dart and twist the loose ends of cotton round pins to secure them. Turn the dart to the inside and pin, matching notches on long darts. Sew towards the point of the dart, back-stitching at the point. Oversew towards the point of dart(Figure 82).

Figure 82

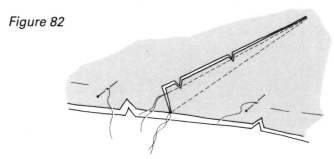

TURNINGS (blue)

Mark the edge of the turning with tailor's chalk (Figure 83a and d). If there is sufficient unsnipped allowance, trim the allowance to make it even, as necessary (Figure 83a). Turn it to the inside along chalk marks (Figure 83b), and sew the hem (Figure 83c). If there is not enough allowance, or if it is snipped (Figure 83d), trim at the chalk marks (Figure 83e) and bind the edge.

To bind, use a straight strip for a straight edge and a bias strip for a shaped edge. Place the right side of the strip to the wrong side of the cover and sew close to the edge (Figure 83f). Turn the strip to the outside and pin, taking care not to turn up the seam allowance inside the binding as this would make the cover too short at this point (Figure 83g). Turn in the raw edge of the strip and sew close to the edge (Figure 83h).

STANDARD STEPS FOR SEWING TACKED SEAMS

Sew the unpiped (blue) seams, completing steps 1, 3, 4, 5 and 6 for each seam before proceeding to the next. Then sew the piped

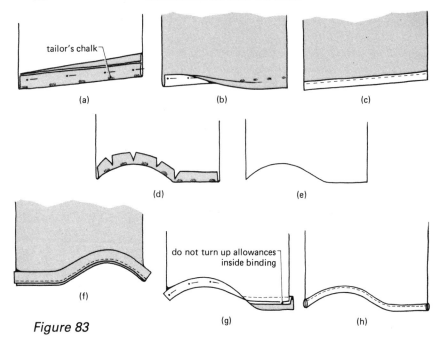

Figure 83

seams, completing steps 1 – 6 for each seam. Sew all seams in the same order as tacked.

1. *Turn.* Undo as little as possible of the adjacent seams in order to get at the seam to be sewn, and twist the loose ends of cotton round pins to secure (see Figure 82). Remove the tacking of the seam to be sewn and turn the pieces to the inside.

2. *Pipe.* Use piping directly from the batch, cutting off the amount you need when almost at the end of the seam.

With the piping foot, sew the piping to the right side of one of the pieces: either the piece that is shaped, the smaller piece when the other has to be eased into the seam at some point, or the piece with no joins. Some examples of the pieces that are usually piped are given in the additional directions for seams which follow the standard steps.

Sew with the edge of the piping allowance level with the edge of the piece. If the piping allowance was trimmed to a regular ½ in (1.25 cm) the piping will establish a consistent, well-shaped seam line with no trouble at all. Do not pull the piping. Ease it on at all times, but especially round curves.

Where there are seams crossing the beginning and/or end of the one you are sewing make the ends of the piping hollow by pulling out the cord, cutting off about ¾ in (2 cm), and letting it spring back inside the casing. You will not then break the machine needle when sewing across the ends of the piping, and if the cord shrinks it will do so without pulling the cover out of shape (Figure 84a).

If the piping starts at a hem or bound edge, open the casing, cut off ½ in (1.25 cm) of cord (Figure 84b), and turn in the casing before sewing (Figure 84c); if it finishes at a hem or bound edge cut off ½ in (1.25 cm) more piping than you need when near the end of the seam, open the casing, cut off ½ in (1.25 cm) of cord (Figure 84d), turn in the casing and continue sewing (Figure 84e).

When piping an outside curve snip the allowance as you go so that it lies flat and is not too tight (Figure 84f); on an inside curve cut out small notches wherever the allowance bunches up (Figure 84g). The same applies to outside and inside angles (Figure 84h and i).

3. *Pin.*   Pin the pieces together with edges even and notches matching. Pin across the seam, in the case of piped seams with the unpiped piece on top. When one of the pieces has to be eased into the seam (like the top of a sleeve into an armhole), distribute the fullness evenly between notches, using lots of pins, and tack (Figure 84j).

4. *Sew.*   Sew unpiped seams ½ in (1.25 cm) from the edge, crossing the pins slowly so as not to break the machine needle; sew piped seams with the unpiped piece on top, removing the pins as you come to them and continually checking that you are sewing on the piping line and not a little outside it.

When a seam begins or ends at a finished edge such as a hem, back-stitch to secure. If a seam crosses the one you are sewing leave gaps as you did in tacking, and complete the seam as soon as the one that crosses is sewn.

You may have noticed that although ⅝ in (1.5 cm) was allowed for seams when trimming, only ½ in (1.25 cm) is taken up in the sewing. This is to provide for shrinkage, and although ⅛ in (3 mm) may not sound much it does give an extra ¼ in (6 mm) per seam all round. This together with the little extra allowed in tuck-in, should be sufficient for reasonable shrinkage.

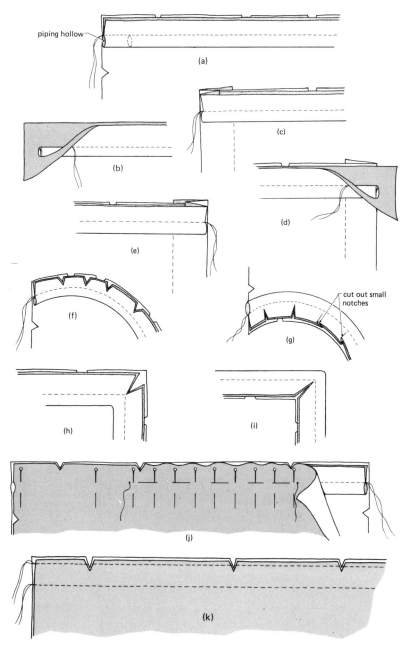

piping hollow

(a)

(b)

(c)

(d)

(e)

(f)

(g)

cut out small
notches

(h)

(i)

(j)

(k)

Figure 84

5. *Oversew.*   These seams are not pressed open so they can be oversewn with allowances together, either with a second line of stitching ⅜ in (1 cm) outside the seam line (Figure 84k), which is quite adequate to prevent fraying, or with a zig-zag attachment if it is sturdy enough for soft furnishing fabrics.

Oversew as soon as each seam is sewn. If this step is left until all the seams are sewn there may be no allowance left to oversew, and there will be parts of the cover which you will be unable to get at.

6. *Trim.*   Trim to neaten only. If a seam allowance looks as if it needs trimming it was probably not sewn correctly. Sometimes the fault is that the piping was sewn more than ½ in (1.25 cm) from the edge, in which case the cover will be too small at this point, and the seam will have to be sewn again using fresh piping, as the former length will be too short. It is more likely, however, that one of the pieces needs to be eased further into the seam.

ADDITIONAL DIRECTIONS FOR PIPED SEAMS

The particular piece that is generally piped is given for each type of seam. Pin and sew the seams as tacked, following the standard steps together with additional directions as appropriate.

BROWN SEAMS – SEAT WITH TUCK-IN

Do not pipe the tuck-in. Before removing the tacking mark the top of the tuck-in each side of the seat with pins (Figure 85a, fireside chair and Figure 85b, armchair/settee). Mark both seam

Figure 85

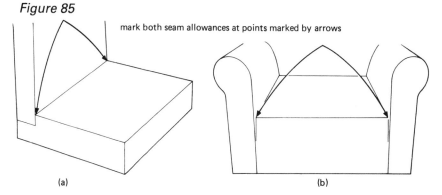

mark both seam allowances at points marked by arrows

(a)   (b)

allowances and use the marks not only to show where the piping should start and finish, but also to match up the pieces exactly at this point when pinning the seam ready for sewing.

TV/fireside chair with front and side borders

Pipe the seat from mark to mark, leaving 1 in (2.5 cm) of loose, hollow casing before the start (Figure 86a) and after the finish. Pin and sew the complete seam, either from the back of the chair (Figure 86b) or the bottom of the tuck-in (Figure 86c) to the

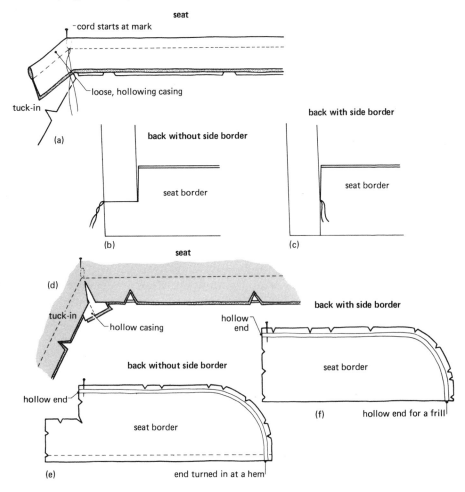

Figure 86

same place on the other side. Trail the loose ends of hollow casing off the seam as you come to them (Figure 86d).

TV/fireside chair with side borders only

If the chair does not have wooden arms pipe the borders from the mark to the bottom of the cover, finishing the ends of the piping as directed in the standard steps; i.e., with a hollow end where the seam will cross and as appropriate at a hem (Figure 86e) or frill (Figure 86f).

Sew the complete seam, either from the back of the chair (Figure 86b) or the bottom of the tuck-in (Figure 86c) to the bottom of the cover.

If the chair has wooden arms the seat will have to be piped instead of the borders. Pipe each side of the seat from the mark to the bottom of the cover, leaving 1 in (2.5 cm) of loose, hollow casing at the mark as shown in Figure 86a. The remaining steps are the same as for a chair without wooden arms.

Note that arms do not affect the continuity of a seat seam. Just keep on sewing across the gaps in the borders (Figure 87).

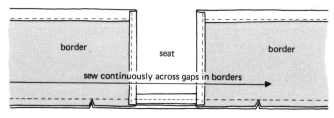

Armchair/settee

Figure 87

Pipe the seat from mark to mark, leaving 1 in (2.5 cm) of loose, hollow casing before the start and after the finish. Figure 88a shows the piping starting at the top of the tuck-in of a seat that is level with the arms; Figure 88b shows the same thing on a seat that protrudes.

Pin and sew the complete seam from the bottom of the tuck-in on one side to the same place on the other side (Figure 88c), trailing the loose ends of hollow casing off the seam as you come to them (see Figure 86d for trailing).

It is important that the stitching of the brown seams and the oversewing should start and finish exactly at the blue seams, and not cross them or catch in their allowances (Figure 88d).

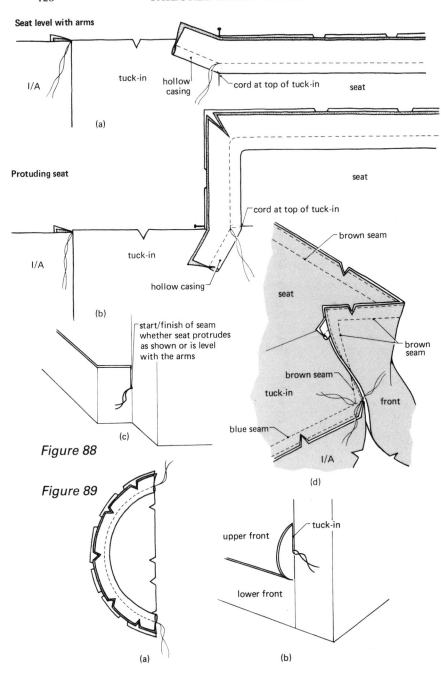

Seat level with arms

tuck-in

hollow casing

cord at top of tuck-in

seat

I/A

(a)

Protuding seat

tuck-in

cord at top of tuck-in

seat

hollow casing

I/A

(b)

start/finish of seam whether seat protrudes as shown or is level with the arms

(c)

brown seam

seat

brown seam

brown seam

tuck-in

front

blue seam

I/A

(d)

Figure 88

Figure 89

(a)

upper front

tuck-in

lower front

(b)

Armchair/settee with rounded front

Pipe the lower front with ends hollow and sew to the upper front. Pipe the curved edges of the side pieces with ends hollow, snipping the piping allowance to ease (Figure 89a). Sew the side pieces to the front, continuing the seam to the bottom of the tuck-in which should not be piped (Figure 89b).

Take care that stitching and oversewing of the brown seams meet the blue seams exactly, and do not cross them nor catch in their allowances (Figure 88d).

BROWN SEAMS – SEAT WITHOUT TUCK-IN

Adjust the stitching and oversewing of the blue seams so that they finish ½ in (1.25 cm) before the end and make fast. Pipe the front and make ends hollow. Sew the seat to the front, ensuring that the ends of the seam meet the ends of the blue seams exactly, without catching in their allowances (Figure 90).

Figure 90

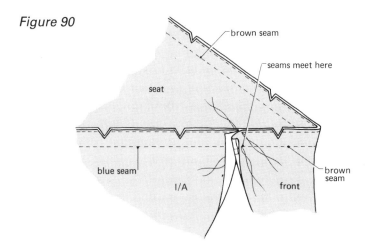

PURPLE SEAMS

Pipe the following pieces of the following seams: the O/A (Figure 75j, k and l); the T/A (Figure 75m and n); the border (Figure 75p and t).

These are straightforward seams which do not need additional directions to the standard steps.

YELLOW SEAMS

Pipe the following pieces of the following seams: F/A (Figure
75b); T/A (Figure 75m and n); F/A and front in one (Figure
75h); inside F/A and border in one (Figure 75p), then the outside
F/A for the F/A-to-O/A seam ; O/A (Figure 75q); O/A and I/A in
one (Figure 75s); top border (Figure 75t), then the O/A, top
border and I/A in one for the front arm seam.

Sew the yellow seams in two directions as tacked, each towards the blue tuck-in seam (Figure 91a and b), or towards the
blue seat seam if there is no tuck-in (Figure 91c). The two parts
of the yellow seam should meet the blue and brown seams
exactly, without crossing or catching in other seam allowances.

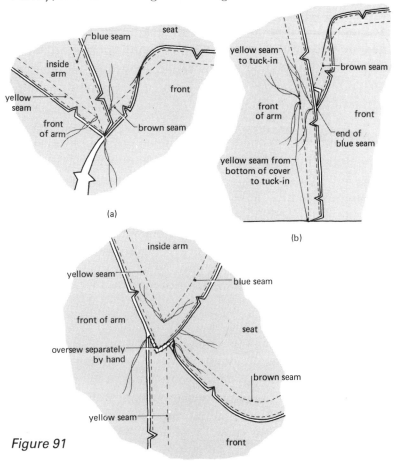

Figure 91

If there is no tuck-in do not oversew by machine beyond the end of the seam line. Oversew the ends of the allowances separately, by hand, as shown in Figure 91c.

GREEN SEAMS (I/B with borders)

Pipe the borders of types as shown in Figure 74b and c unless there are wooden arms, in which case there is no alternative but to pipe the I/B. Pipe the I/B of chairs such as Figure 74d.

Pipe the borders of types shown in Figure 75w and y, and the I/B of types as in Figure 75x.

These are straightforward seams which do not need additional directions to the standard steps.

RED SEAMS

Mark the top of an opening before removing the tacking of the seam. On all chairs pipe the O/B, including opening(s), taking the piping along the line of chalk marks to the bottom of the cover.

Pin and sew, excluding opening(s), as directed in the standard steps.

GREEN SEAMS (I/B and wings or I/B and arms)

Pipe the following pieces: the border of a wing inside seam (Figure 75z); O/Ws and O/B in one (Figure 74i and 75c); O/B and O/As in one (Figure 75d and aa).

Chair with wings

Where blue and green seams meet under a wing, fold the allowances away from each other. These seams should meet the purple seam at the same point, side-by-side (Figure 92a). If the arm only goes as far as the wing the allowance of the green seam should be folded towards the back of the chair and that of the blue seam towards the front of the chair (Figure 92b).

ALL SEAMS

Make a final check that all seams are sewn, especially the gaps that were left where seams crossed.

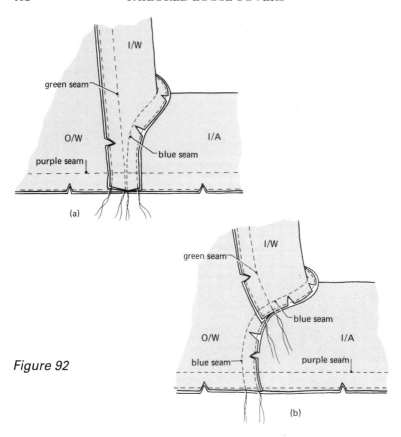

Figure 92

FASTENINGS FOR CHAIR/SETTEE OPENINGS

Hooks and eyes

Cut a 2 in (5 cm)-wide straight strip twice the length of the opening for a frilled cover, plus 2 in (5 cm) for hems for a plain-tailored cover. Stitch a narrow hem at the outside, also double ½ in (1.25 cm) hems at each end if the cover is plain-tailored. Sew the strip to the opening, right-sides-together, from the bottom of the cover up to meet the seam each side. Oversew and trim to neaten (Figure 93a). Turn the facing to the inside and sew the outside edge on the piped side to the cover, from the bottom up. Sew hooks on the piped side, eyes on the other (Figure 93b).

Hook and eyelet tape

Cut the required length (the length of the opening plus 1 in (2.5 cm)) so that there is ½ in (1.25 cm) of plain tape at top and bottom. With the piping foot, sew the hook tape to the seam allowance on the piped side, starting about ¼ in (6 mm) above

Figure 93

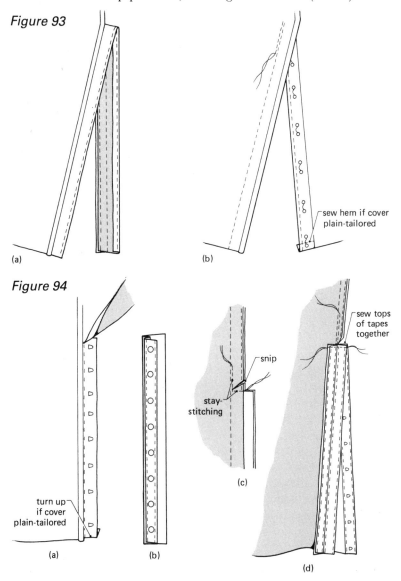

sew hem if cover
plain-tailored

(a)   (b)

Figure 94

sew tops
of tapes
together

snip

stay-
stitching

turn up
if cover
plain-tailored

(a)   (b)   (c)   (d)

the opening. If the cover is plain-tailored turn under the bottom of the tape as you stitch (Figure 94a). Sew the eyelet tape to the right side of a 2½ in (6.5 cm)-wide straight strip, allowing ½ in (1.25 cm) for a seam at the inside and turning the outside edge under the tape (Figure 94b). Sew the strip to the other side of the opening, matching eyelets with hooks. Oversew and trim to neaten. Stay-stitch the corner of the allowance above the opening and snip diagonally almost to the stitching (Figure 94c). Hook up the tapes at the top and sew the tops together securely (Figure 94d). Sew the outside of the hook tape to the cover from the bottom up (Figure 93b).

Zip fastener
Follow the directions enclosed with the fastener.

SKIRTS AND FRILLS

Carefully trim round the bottom of the cover by cutting where marked. Pipe ½ in (1.25 cm) from the edge, turning in the ends of the casing at the opening. (Piping is optional for skirts, which sometimes look better without.)

Note that by cutting at the marks instead of ½ in (1.25 cm) below them to allow for the seam, the length of the cover is shortened by this amount. This is to prevent the skirt or frill from dragging on the floor and catching under castors.

Skirts

Plain skirt. Cut the number of widths estimated. Cut widths into half-widths or assemble wide pieces as appropriate. Wide pieces for the front and back of a settee should be assembled the same as for the seat of the cover, by sewing part-widths to each side of a full width.

Pin the pieces to the cover right-sides-together and centre-to-centre (Figure 95a). If the material is patterned choose the best-looking piece for the front.

Trim the width of the pieces as necessary, allowing for double ½ in (1.25 cm) hems each side. The pieces should meet closely at the corners but not overlap. Stitch 1 in (2.5 cm) bottom hems with ½ in (1.25 cm) turned in, then stitch the side hems. Sew the pieces to the cover in one continuous seam. Oversew and trim to neaten (Figure 95b). Press the seam upwards.

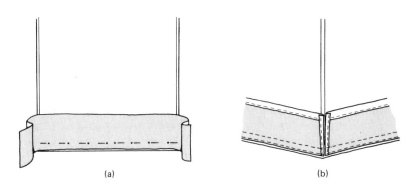

(a)   (b)

Figure 95

Skirt with corner pleats.   Proceed as for a plain skirt as far as pinning the pieces to the cover (Figure 95a).

On the inside, pin 4 in (10 cm) pleats each side of a corner, if possible taking one piece round the back of the pleats to join the other at the inside fold, out of sight. Trim at the join, allowing for a ½ in (1.25 cm) seam, and tack the pleats in place. Pin and tack the pleats at the other corners in the same way. Sew a 1 in (2.5 cm) bottom hem with ½ in (1.25 cm) turned in, then sew and oversew the joins. Sew the skirt to the cover and oversew. Note that if a piece has to be added to make up the required width, it should be joined at the inside folds of the pleats (Figure 96).

Figure 96

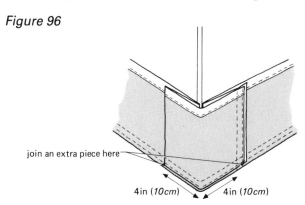

join an extra piece here

4 in (*10 cm*)   4 in (*10 cm*)

Frills

First join together any pieces obtained from trimmings, then cut
the number of widths estimated for the frill less whatever you
have acquired from trimmings. Oversew the raw edges of joins
separately (not with allowances together as on the cover).

Box-pleated frill.   On the right side, mark the top of the frill at 2
in (5 cm) intervals. Fold the second mark back to the first and
pin, the third forward to the fourth and pin, and so on (Figure
97a). Hide the joins inside the pleats where possible and press
open those that cannot be hidden. Stay-stitch the pleats ⅜ in (1
cm) from the edge. Pin the frill to the cover right-sides-together,
arranging for a space to fall at each of the front corners and an
extra 2 in (5 cm) of unpleated frill at the beginning and end.

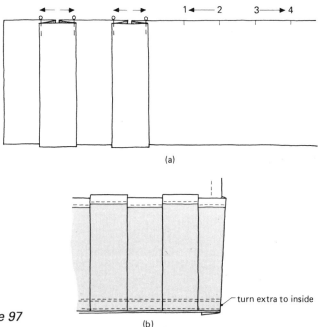

(a)

turn extra to inside

Figure 97

(b)

Turn under ½ in (1.25 cm) at each end and stitch, then fold
the remaining extra material to the inside of the cover to form
facings. Sew the frill to the cover and oversew, back-stitching at
beginning and end. Sew a 1 in (2.5 cm) bottom hem with ½ in
(1.25 cm) turned in (Figure 97b).

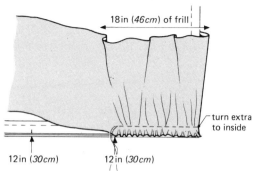

Figure 98

Gathered frill. Mark the bottom of the cover at 12 in (30 cm) intervals. Turn under ½ in (1.25 cm) and edge stitch at the beginning of the frill. Pin the frill to the cover right-sides-together, with 1½ in (4 cm) turned to the inside to form a facing. Measure 18 in (46 cm) of frill and pin to the 12 in (30 cm) mark on the cover. Gather the frill to fit, and tack it to the cover, arranging the gathers evenly (Figure 98). Continue gathering in this way, finishing with a 1½ in (4 cm) facing as at the beginning. Sew the frill to the cover, back-stitching at beginning and end, and oversew. Sew a 1 in (2.5 cm) bottom hem with ½ in (1.25 cm) turned in.

FINISHING TOUCHES

Press the cover well with a steam iron. At the same time generally neaten the seams and check again that all are sewn and oversewn.

TV/fireside chairs with wooden arms

If the arms interrupt seat borders tuck a length of ½ in (1.25 cm) tape into the side hem of each border (sufficient to tie round the arm) and sew (Figure 99).

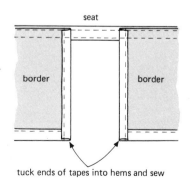

Figure 99

tuck ends of tapes into hems and sew

Upholstered arms with wooden tops

Line the top borders with ¼ in (6 mm)-thick foam, cut to the length and width of the arm. Sew it loosely by hand to the seam allowances.

Flaps on plain-tailored covers

Thread tape through the slots in the flaps and tie under the chair (Figure 100).

Figure 100

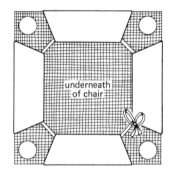

Frilled covers

Cut four lengths of tape, each sufficient to tie round a leg. Fold each length in half and sew it to the seam allowance of the frill at each corner.

CUSHIONS

The sewing of the cushions is much the same whether the cover has been fitted or shaped from measurements. If the former, undo as little tacking as necessary to remove the piece to be worked on, and take care to marry up the notches properly when pinning the pieces right-sides-together.

Pinned seams on one-and-a-half- and two-width divan cushion covers

Sew the joins in the top, bottom, front border and back border as directed for pinned seams for settee backs and seats (Figure 80).

Piping tops and bottoms

Make up piping as directed on pages 116–18 and trim the allowance to ½ in (1.25 cm) *exactly*. Pipe (i.e. sew the piping to) the following pieces as appropriate:

Boxed cushions.   Pipe the top and bottom.

Cushions boxed at sides only.   This type is shown in Figure 25f. First sew the top to the bottom at the front with a ½ in (1.25 cm) seam. Oversew the allowances and press the seam open (Figure 102). Pipe the combined top and bottom.

Unboxed cushions.   These are shown in Figure 25d and l. Pipe the top.

Start at the back of the piece and pipe all round, keeping the edge of the piping allowance level with the edge of the piece. Sew loosely and snip at the corners and/or curves to ease. When a few inches from where you started cut the amount of piping required plus 1 in (2.5 cm) (Figure 101a). Unpick the ends of the casing, join them with a ½ in (1.25 cm) seam, and cut off the surplus cord (Figure 101b). Sew the join to the piece.

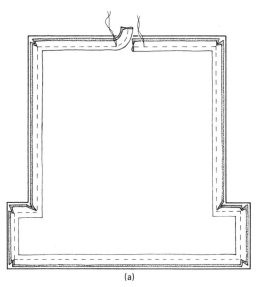

(a)

Figure 101

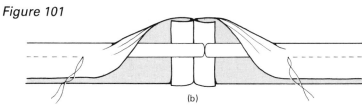

(b)

Note that as the piping allowance has been trimmed to a regular ½ in (1.25 cm), a well-shaped seam will be established quite easily; also, since only ½ in (1.25 cm) is taken up of the ⅝ in (1.5 cm) allowed for seams, a little extra is provided all round in case of shrinkage.

Assembling covers made from measurements

Pin one set of border pieces to a top and bottom (front and back of a stand-up cushion – see instructions in brackets throughout). Pin the pieces right-sides-together, ensuring that the material is running from the back to the front of the cushion (top to bottom of a stand-up cushion).

Chair/settee cushion.   Front (top) border: Pin to the top and bottom, centre-to-centre. *Side borders*: Pin from front to back (top to bottom), allowing for a seam at the front (top). Pin the side borders to the front border. *Back (bottom) opening*: Pin to the top and bottom, centre-to-centre. Take the opening round the sides, snipping the allowance of the opening at the corners to ease, and pin it to the side borders. Do not trim the width of the side borders or opening as yet; leave whatever extra there may be at the seams, as shown in Figure 73b and c.

Cushion with side borders only.   If the borders are shaped at the front, mark one border as directed on page 91 (Figure 61c) and cut to shape ⅝ in (1.5 cm) outside the marking. Cut the second border from the first. Pin in the directions shown in Figure 102, then pin a back opening the same as for the above cushion.

Divan cushion.   Front border: Pin to the top and bottom, centre-to-centre. *Side border*: Pin to the top and bottom, centre-to-centre, and pin to the front border. *Back border*: Pin to the top and bottom, centre-to-centre, to within 7–8 in (17–20 cm) of the end with the opening. Pin to the side border. *Side opening*: Pin from front to back, allowing for the seam at the front, and pin to the front border. Pin the opening round the back, snipping the allowance of the opening to ease at the corner, and pin to the back border. Do not trim the width of the back border or opening as yet; leave whatever extra there may be at the seam, as shown in Figure 73b and c.

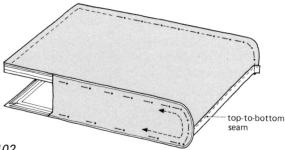

top-to-bottom
seam

Figure 102

All cushions

Open the opening and try the cover wrong-side-out on the cushion. Adjust the width of the opening as necessary at the opening-to-border seams, so that the cover can be put on and removed without strain. Remove the cover and trim the opening-to-border seams to the seam allowance.

Unpin the opening from the assembled cushion. Trim all alike openings to the same width, and finish as follows:

Hand-sewn hooks and eyes.   Sew the pinned hems. Sew hooks and eyes at 2 in (5 cm) intervals along the middle of the hems – hooks on the inside of the upper piece, eyes on the outside of the lower piece.

Hook and eyelet tape.   Turn under ⅜ in (1 cm) at the bottom of the upper piece and sew hook tape ⅛ in (3 mm) from the edge on the inside (Figure 103a). Turn ½ in (1.25 cm) to the outside at the top of the lower piece and stitch eyelet tape to the edge on the outside (Figure 103b).

Figure 103

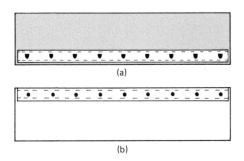

(a)

(b)

Zip fastener.   Insert in the usual way, taking up ½ in (1.25 cm) turnings.

All openings.   Do up the hooks and eyes or close the zip. Stay-stitch ¾ in (2 cm) from the edge at the sides and trim to neaten (Figure 104).

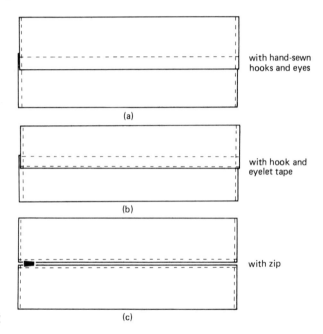

(a)   with hand-sewn hooks and eyes

(b)   with hook and eyelet tape

(c)   with zip

Figure 104

Replace the opening on the assembled cushion and assemble other alike cushions in the same way. When making covers for reversed shapes (Figure 61g), ensure that the overlapping part of the opening is facing away from the top (front) in each case.

Sewing assembled/fitted covers

Chair/settee/divan cushions.   Sew the corner border seams, oversew the allowances separately and press the seams open. Sew opening-to-border seams, oversew with the allowances together and press the seams away from the opening. Sew the border to the top (front) and oversew with the allowances together (Figure 105); then sew the border to the bottom (back) in the same way. Trim the finished cover to neaten.

Cushions with side borders only.   Sew in the same directions as pinned and trim to neaten (Figure 106).

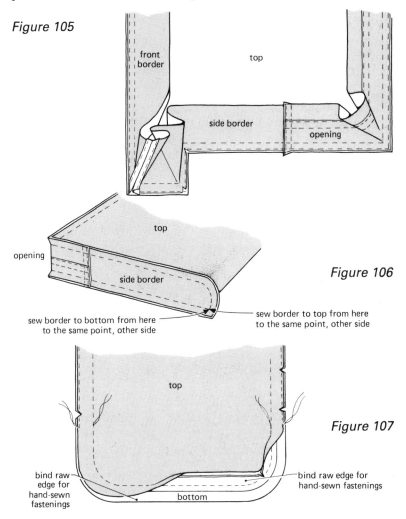

Figure 105

front border

top

side border

opening

top

opening

side border

Figure 106

sew border to bottom from here to the same point, other side

sew border to top from here to the same point, other side

top

Figure 107

bind raw edge for hand-sewn fastenings

bind raw edge for hand-sewn fastenings

bottom

Sewing covers without borders

Sew the top to the bottom as far as the opening. Oversew with the allowances together and trim to neaten (Figure 107). Finish the opening with a zip; or bind the allowances with bias strips and sew on hooks and eyes by hand every 2 in (5 cm); or sew on hook and eyelet tape, adapting the directions given on page 141.

7
UNUSUAL FEATURES

These directions either modify or supplement those in the main sections. It is therefore recommended that you make a straightforward cover before attempting one with an unusual feature.

SETTEE I/B IN THREE SECTIONS WITH RECESSES

Sections with recesses are individually sprung and must therefore be covered with three separate pieces.

Estimating

Refer to the introduction to estimating, pages 22–6, and to the sample estimating and cutting list, page 27. Estimate for the inside back first, then for the seat and front.

Inside back.   Since tuck-in is required inside each recess, it is most unlikely that half widths could be used for the sections. It is therefore unnecessary to measure the width to work out the number of widths required. *Enter 3 widths in column 4 of your list.*
Measure the longest section where it is longest (Figure 108), add 1 in (2.5 cm) for the seam and 4 in (10 cm) for the seat tuck-in, and enter in column 3 of your list. Note: Include a top border in the measurement and add 2″ for a tuck seam (Figure 109).
Estimate by multiplying the length (column 3) by the number of widths (column 4) and enter it in column 5.

Seat and front.   **Measure** the width of the S & F where it is widest (Figure 108), add 2 in (5 cm) for seams and enter in column 2 of your list.

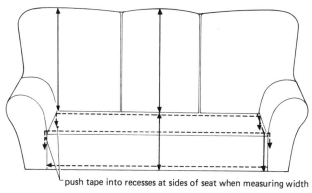

push tape into recesses at sides of seat when measuring width

Figure 108

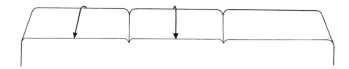

Figure 109

Measure the length of the S & F where it is longest (Figure 108), add 4 in (10 cm) for seat tuck-in, 2 in (5 cm) for tuck-seam, and 2 in (5 cm) for a hem if the cover is plain-tailored, and enter in column 3 of your list.

Estimate by entering the appropriate number of widths in column 4 of your list and multiplying out to column 5.

S & F up to 48 in (122 cm) wide, including allowances: 1 width

S & F more than 48 in (122 cm) wide, including allowances: 2 widths. If the width is no more than 72 in (183 cm), reserve a half width × the length of the S & F.

Cutting, and placing and fitting

Refer to the introduction to cutting and placing, pages 48–51; and to fitting, page 94.

Inside back. Cut widths in plain material as directed in the introduction. Centre a patterned material as directed on page 51 for chairs with boxed cushions (Figure 29) and match the two further widths as shown on page 53 (Figure 31). Place the pieces

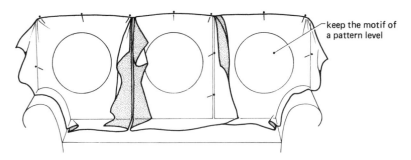

keep the motif of
a pattern level

Figure 110

centre-to-centre on the sections, ensuring that the motif of a patterned material is level on all three (Figure 110).

Pin tuck-seams at a top border and cut them open (Figure 37b and c for tuck seams). Straighten the border pieces, pin the joins and trim to size (Figure 111).

Figure 111

Pin tuck-seams each side of the recesses and cut them open. Trim the pieces of material between the tuck-seams to the depth of the recess plus ⅝ in (1.5 cm) for a seam, and pin these pieces together. Figure 112a shows the tuck-in expanded; Figure 112b shows the tuck-in outside the recess. Push the tuck-ins into the recesses to check that the joins do not pull the cover out of shape, and adjust if necessary.

Seat and front. Cut the widths for the S & F. A patterned material does not have to be centred on the seat unless there are no boxed cushions (see page 51 for chairs without boxed cushions). However, if two widths are required they must match. Cut one width into part widths and join to the full width as directed on pages 56–8.

Pin up a bottom hem if necessary and pin the bottom of the piece to the bottom of the front, centre-to-centre. Smooth the material to the back of the seat and pin the sides of the front to the settee. Pin a tuck-seam at the front and trim the sides of the seat as shown in Figure 39f.

Join the S & F to the I/B (Figure 113), allowing the tuck-ins between the sections to hang free.

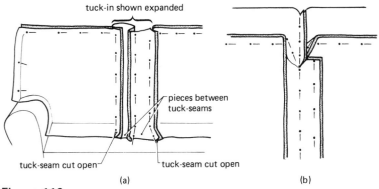

Figure 112

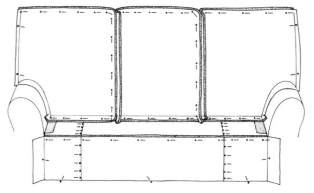

Figure 113

Tacking

Refer to the introduction on preparing, page 108, and tack in the following order:

Inside back.   Blue: Four seams joining the border pieces (Figure 114) and two seams joining the tuck-in recesses (Figure 115).
Green: Centre section: Two side seams, from bottom to top of the recess; top seam from the centre out to the same point each side

Figure 114

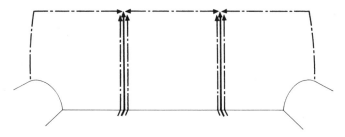

Figure 115

(Figure 115). *Each outside section*: Side seam from bottom to top of the recess; seam from the arm to the same point (Figure 115).

Seat and Front. Blue: Seat-to-I/B seam as pinned, with the tuck-ins hanging free. *Brown:* Front seat seam as directed on page 111.

Sewing

Refer to the standard steps on pages 121–5. Sew in the following order:

Blue seams (unpiped). Sew the four joins in the border, oversew the allowances and press the seams open. Sew the two tuck-in seams at the recesses and oversew with the allowances together.

Green seams (piped). Note that all the green seams should converge *exactly* at the meeting point above each recess. They should not cross each other by one stitch or catch in any other seam allowances. It will not matter if the border seam is slightly off-centre, however. The meeting point automatically establishes itself at the bottom of the shaping regardless of this seam (Figure 116).

   Centre section: Sew the piping to the section from the bottom up one side, across the top and down the other side, all in one piece.

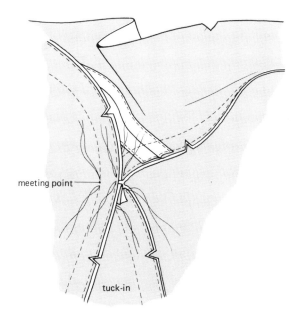

meeting point

tuck-in

Figure 116

Sew the tuck-in to the section each side in the same direction as
tacked (Figure 115) and oversew. Sew the top border to the
section in the same direction as tacked (Figure 115) and oversew.

Each outside section: Sew the piping to the section from the arm
up to the top, across the top and down the side, all in one piece.
Sew the tuck-in to the section in the same direction as tacked
(Figure 115) and oversew. Sew the side and top border to the
section in the same direction as tacked (Figure 115) and oversew.

Top of recess tuck-in. Taper the top 2 in (5 cm) or so of the
tuck-ins, allowing for a seam at the meeting point. Sew and
oversew towards the meeting point (Figure 117).

Seat and front. Sew the seams joining part-widths as shown in
Figure 80, then sew the S & F to the I/B, allowing the tuck-ins to
hang free. Oversew the seam. Bind the ends of tuck-ins, or
oversew them. Sew the piped brown seam as applicable, from the
directions on page 127.

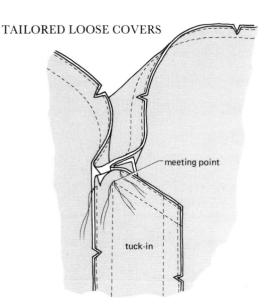

Figure 117

THE OUTSIDE ROLL OF A CHESTERFIELD

Normally the I/A and O/A have to join halfway down the roll arm because the back of the O/A is not as rounded as the front, and an under-roll seam would sag at the back. This is not the case with a chesterfield, where the shaping is the same all round the outside.

Estimating

Try the width of the roll where it is plumpest when measuring for the widest part of the I/B and the I/As. Take the tape to the bottom of the roll when measuring the lengths of the I/B, O/B, I/As and O/As (Figure 118).

Cutting and placing

If using a patterned material ensure that the inside arms match the I/B, so that the same motif shows at the same level all round the inside of the settee.

Fitting

Extend the I/B-to-I/A seams to the bottom of the roll (Figure 119).

Tacking

Leave gaps in the yellow seams where the under-roll seam meets.

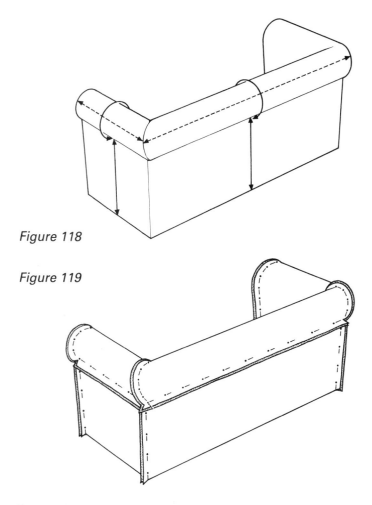

Figure 118

Figure 119

Leave the under-roll seam to the last and tack in a colour not used elsewhere on the cover, from one side of the front to the other.

Sewing

Sew and oversew in the same order as tacked. The I/A-to-I/B seams are not piped, but the O/A-to-O/B seams (red) are piped in the usual way. Pipe the under-roll seam, sewing the piping to the O/As and O/B in one. Sew the seam as tacked. Sew up the gaps in yellow seams.

CHAIR WITH REMOVABLE ARMS

Remove the arms when estimating and fitting the chair cover and make this as directed in the relevant main sections.

Allow for tuck-in at the sides of the seat if necessary and join the sides to the O/As, leaving gaps where the arms slot in. Oversew the gaps with several lines of stay-stitching.

Estimating

It is not usually necessary to estimate for the parts of the arms that fit inside the chair as these can be covered out of trimmings. (There will be trimmings from the chair cover as well as from the pieces estimated for the arm covers, if the latter are more than 24 in (61 cm) wide).

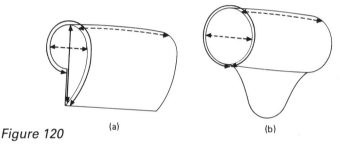

Figure 120   (a)   (b)

Measure the outside part of the body and one end where these pieces are widest and longest (Figure 120a or b). Add 2 in (5 cm) for seams to each measurement and estimate per pair of arms;

Up to 24 in (61 cm) wide: 1 width × length of body, and
                               1 width × length of end (sufficient
                               for 4 ends and piping).

More than 24 in (61 cm) wide: 2 widths × length of body (sufficient
                               also for ends and piping).

Cutting

Cut the number of widths estimated and trim the pieces to size as directed in the main sections, remembering to keep a large pattern motif central.

Fitting

Pin one body piece and two ends right-side-out on an arm and trim the ends roughly to shape. Fill in the inside of the arm from trimmings, leaving a gap for whatever attaches the arm to the chair.

Pin the pieces together and take out the pins holding the material to the arm (Figure 121).

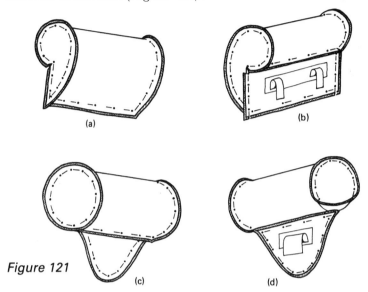

(a)

(b)

Figure 121

(c)

(d)

Mark an opening at the bottom of the arm by parting the seam and rubbing tailor's chalk over the pins (Figure 122). Remove the pins where marked and try to take off the cover.

Unfortunately, the opening usually has to be extended to an end seam in order to get the cover off. Mark and remove a few pins at the back end of the cover, on the inside if possible, and ease it off. If there is any strain mark and remove a few more

Figure 122

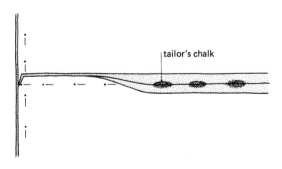

tailor's chalk

pins, and so on until the cover will go on and off easily. Figure 123 shows the extent of the average opening.

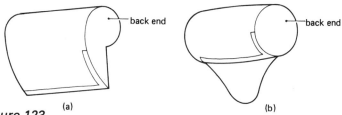

Figure 123   (a)   (b)

Preparing

Trim and notch the cover in the usual way except for the openings, which should be trimmed to a ½ in (1.25 cm) allowance from the chalk marks.

Unpin the cover and use the pieces as a pattern for cutting other alike arm covers to shape.

Sewing

First bind the edges of the opening as follows: sew a 2 in (5 cm) wide strip to the cover right-sides-together along the line of chalk marks; turn the strip to the inside, turn under ½ in (1.25 cm) and sew along the line of chalk marks.

Bind a straight opening with straight strips. If the opening extends round an end, bind the edge of the body that extends with a bias strip and mitre the corner as shown in Figure 124; bind the edge that does not extend with a straight strip.

Finish a gap for an arm attachment with several lines of stay-stitching.

Pipe the ends, leaving ¾ in (2 cm) of hollow casing at the start and finish on the type in Figure 125a. (See page 123 for making piping hollow). Join the piping on the type in Figure 125b as shown on page 139.

Pin the body to the ends, right-sides-together with notches matching. Sew the seams and oversew with the allowances together.

Bind the allowances of the piped part of the opening. Sew hooks at 1 in (2.5 cm) intervals on the side of the opening with the piped edge, with eyes to match on the other side.

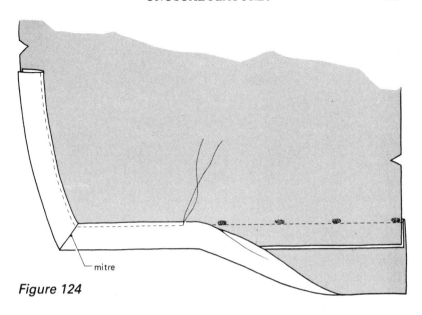

mitre

Figure 124

Figure 125

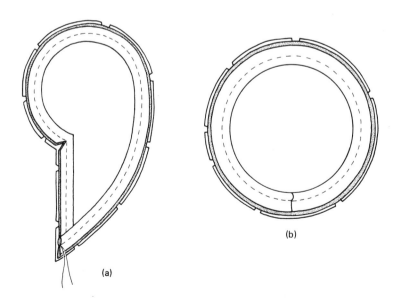

(a)

(b)

BOLSTER ARMS

A pattern should run from front to back of a round bolster, when width and length are measured as shown in Figure 126a. On a square bolster it should run from the outside to the seat, and width and length should be measured as shown in Figure 126b.

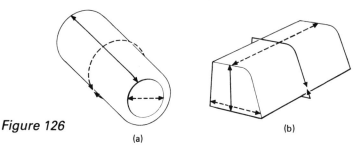

Figure 126

(a)   (b)

Estimating

Add allowances for seams as follows:

Round Bolster: 2 in (5 cm) to all measurements.
Square Bolster: 2 in (5 cm) to width, 4 in (10 cm) to length of body;
2 in (5 cm) to width and length of end.
    Estimate per pair, according to width plus allowances:
Body up to 24 in (61 cm) wide: 1 width × length of arm
Body more than 24 in (61 cm) wide: 2 widths × length of arm.
    Check if there are suitable trimmings for the ends from the chair/settee cover, and if not estimate:
4 ends up to 12 in (30 cm) wide: 1 width × length of end
4 ends more than 12 in (30 cm) wide: 2 widths × length of end.

Cutting

Cut the number of widths estimated and trim the pieces to size in the usual way, ensuring that a distinct pattern motif is central and well shown.
    Cut the top and bottom of a square bolster separately (Figure 127a). Cut the top first, centring a pattern between the outside top and inside bottom of the bolster, and allowing above the motif for the top to extend down the outside, plus seam (Figure 127b); then cut the bottom, allowing for seams.

Squashy bolster. If a bolster is too squashy to be fitted in the usual way, shape the ends from measurements as follows. Mea-

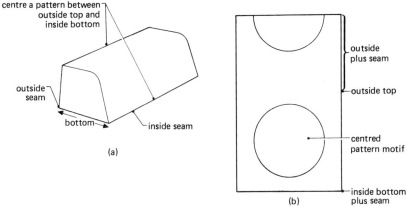

Figure 127

sure half the diameter plus ⅝ in (1.5 cm) from the centre of the piece out to one corner and mark with tailor's chalk (Figure 128a). Measure and mark several times each side of the first mark, then join up the marks (Figure 128b) and trim to that shape. Use this corner as a pattern for cutting the other corners (Figure 128c). The fully trimmed piece can then be used as a pattern for cutting other ends.

Figure 128

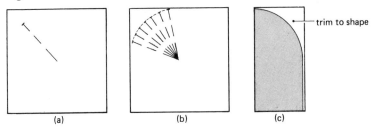

Fitting

Firm bolster. Pin a set of pieces right-side-out on one arm and trim the ends roughly to shape. Pin the pieces together, snipping the body allowance as necessary to ease. Take out the pins holding the material to the arm (Figure 129).

Mark the seam joining the body piece (the outside seam of a square bolster) for an opening, by parting the seam and rubbing tailor's chalk over the pins (Figure 122). Remove the marked pins and take off the cover

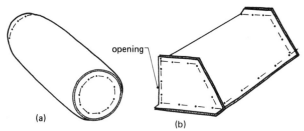

Figure 129

Squashy bolster.   First pipe the ends as this makes it easier to pin the pieces together. Pipe as shown in Figure 125b.

Pin the body piece to the ends right-sides-together; keep the body piece loose and snip the allowance to ease as you pin (Figure 130a). Pin the join of the body piece, taking up a ½ in (1.25 cm) seam (Figure 130b).

Figure 130

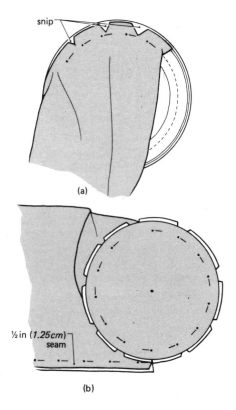

Preparing

Trim and notch the cover in the usual way except for the opening. Trim the opening of a fitted cover to ½ in (1.25 cm) from the chalk marks.

Unpin the cover and use the pieces as a pattern for cutting other covers. Cut for alike bolster arms with 'pattern' and piece right-sides-together; cut for opposite arms with wrong side of 'pattern' to wrong side of material.

Sewing

Either bind the opening edges for hand-sewn hooks and eyes as shown in Figure 124 or use hook and eyelet tape, adapting the directions given in the main section on page 132.

Pipe the ends of a cover for a firm arm as directed Figure 125b. The method is the same whether the end is round or square.

Sew the body to the ends right-sides-together with notches matching. Oversew the seams with the allowances together.

BOLSTER ARMS AND BACK UNIT

Estimating

Measure as shown in Figure 131 and add 2 in (5 cm) for seams to each measurement. Estimate for width plus allowances:
Arms up to 24 in (61 cm) wide: 1 width × length of arm
Arms more than 24 in (61 cm) wide: 2 widths × length of arm
Back up to 48 in (122 cm) wide: 1 width × length of back
Back more than 48 in (122 cm) wide: 2 widths × length of back
Two ends: Chek if these can be obtained from trimmings, either from the settee cover or from the pieces estimated above. If not, estimate 1 width × length of end.

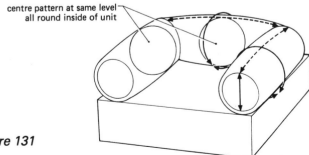

centre pattern at same level
all round inside of unit

Figure 131

Cutting and Placing

Cut the number of widths estimated and trim the pieces to size in the usual way, ensuring that a pattern is centred on the inside of the unit at the same level all round as shown in Figure 131. As the body pieces join at the centre underneath the unit, allow above the centred motif for the pieces to extend round the back to this point; also allow below the motif for the pieces to extend to the same point (Figure 132).

Figure 132

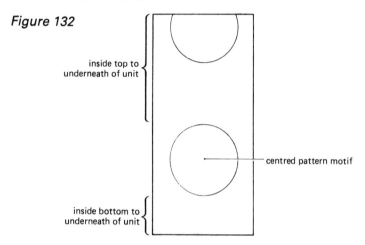

inside top to underneath of unit

centred pattern motif

inside bottom to underneath of unit

If the back is more than 48 in (122 cm) wide, cut part widths and join them to each side of the full width as directed on pages 56–8. Trim the piece equally at the sides to the width of the back at its widest point, plus allowances.

Pin the pieces right-sides-out on the unit with the body pieces joining at the centre underneath. Trim the ends roughly to shape.

Fitting

Pin the pieces together and trim as necessary, allowing more than enough for seams (Figure 133). Mark an opening in the underneath seam by rubbing tailor's chalk over the pins (Figure 122). The opening will probably need to extend all the way across the back and about 12 in (30 cm) along each arm. Try this length and if it is not sufficient keep marking and removing pins until the cover can be taken off without strain.

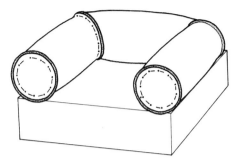

Figure 133

Preparing

Trim and notch in the usual way except for the opening, which should be trimmed to ½ in (1.25 cm) from the chalk marks.

Tacking and sewing

First, either bind the edges of the opening for hand-sewn hooks and eyes as shown in Figure 124, or sew on hook and eyelet tape, adapting the directions given on page 132.

Tack, sew and oversew the seams in the usual way, in the following order:

Arm-to-back seams:	Piping is optional but generally they look better without.
Underneath seam each side of the opening:	Unpiped
End-to-body seams:	Pipe ends as directed on page 154 (Figure 125b). Sew ends to body and oversew.

8
SMALL COVERS

Refer to introductions to various stages as necessary:

ARM CAPS

Arm caps are well worth making as they will hide or protect the parts of the chair that get the most wear and tear. They are also useful over loose covers, when the need to launder the covers is cut by at least a third.

Caps over patterned loose covers

Do not use a different pattern from that of the covers. When using the same pattern match the caps to the arms, so that the good work put into centring and matching the arms is not obscured.

If it proves too wasteful, and therefore expensive, to match caps and covers, use a plain material that picks out the main colour of the pattern. The effect will be better than a jumble of unmatched pattern.

Caps over plain/self-patterned/all-over patterned covers

You can keep the caps unobtrusive by using the same material or, in the case of plain and self-patterned covers, you can make a feature of them by using a colourful, all-over pattern. (A pattern with a distinct motif would need to be centred and matched on each arm, which would entail extra work and material).

Suggested size of caps

The front of the cap should be about 8–10 in (20–25 cm) long on an averaged-sized arm, and the outside should continue at the same level as the front.

To keep the cap firmly in place the inside should extend to the seat if there is a boxed cushion; to the bottom of the recess at the side of the seat if there is not. (In the Figures that follow the length of the inside is implied by the piping and measurement marks, Figure 134f being an example of a cap for a chair without a boxed cushion.)

The length of the outside of the cap is determined by the length of the front, since it finishes at the same level.

The width of the body is optional but one width cut into half widths provides a pair of pieces suitable for most arms, giving a finished width of about 21 in (53 cm) on most types of arms. On Figure 134d, e and i, the finished width of the body would be several inches less, however, because the outside of the cap extends round the front of the arm, but it would be adequate for this type of arm. Note that in fixing the width of the body in this way, the estimating and cutting is made a lot easier.

Estimating

Mark the front of the arm at the required length for the finished cap.

Front or top arm. For types as in Figure 134a, b, c, f, g and h, measure width and length where the front is widest and longest and add:

Width: 2 in (5 cm) for seams

Length: F/A (Figure 134a, b, c and g): 1 in (2.5 cm) for seam and 2 in (5 cm) for hem

T/A (Figure 134 f and h): 24 in (61 cm) for top and 2 in (5 cm) for hem.

Estimate as appropriate for width and allowances:

F/A or T/A up to 12 in (30 cm) wide: 1 width × length measurement for 1 or 2 pairs; add 9 in (23 cm) for piping if making 2 pairs. 2 widths for 3 pairs.

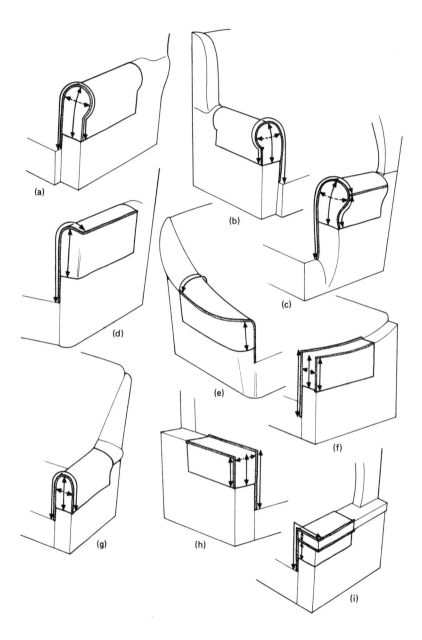

Figure 134

F/A or T/A more than 12 in (30 cm) wide: 1 width × length measurement per pair.

Example: If a T/A measures with allowances say 10 in (25 cm) (width) × 34 in (86 cm) (length), estimate for 1 pair, 34 in (86 cm); 2 pairs, 43 in (109 cm); 3 pairs, 2 widths × 34 in (86 cm) = 68 in (173 cm).

One-piece body. For types as in Figure 134a, b and g, measure the length of the body and add 4 in (10 cm) for hems. Estimate 1 width × this measurement per pair. Note that if the cap is to go over a loose cover, the body of a roll arm should be made in two pieces as shown in Figure 134c, with the outside seam in the same place as on the cover.

Two-piece body. For types as in Figure 134c, d, e, f, h and i, measure the length of the inside and add 1 in (2.5 cm) for a seam, 2 in (5 cm) for the hem. Estimate 1 width × this measurement per pair. Estimate for the outside in the same way.

Border. For types as in Figure 134i, measure the length and add 2 in (5 cm) for seams. Estimate 1 width × this measurement per pair of caps.

Cutting

F/A or T/A. Cut the number of widths estimated. Cut pieces to the width plus allowances of F/A or T/A using the type of layout

Pieces 12 in (30 cm) wide

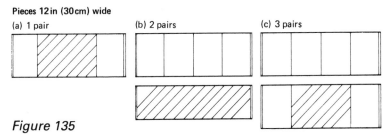

(a) 1 pair   (b) 2 pairs   (c) 3 pairs

Figure 135

shown in Figure 135 for pieces up to 12 in (30 cm) wide; use the layout in Figure 136 for pieces more than 12 in (30 cm) wide.

Pieces more than 12 in (30 cm) wide

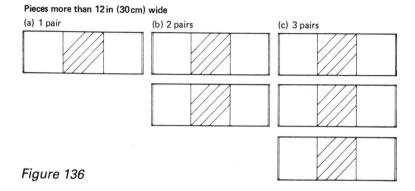

Figure 136

Body. Cut the number of widths estimated and cut widths into half widths.

Piping. Cut bias strips as directed on page 116.

Fitting

Pin a set of pieces right-side-out on a left arm and trim a F/A roughly to shape, allowing more than enough for the seam.

Pin the pieces together, fitting small, short darts as necessary to dispose of fullness. Snip to ease the body round curves (Figure 137a to e). Take out the pins holding the material to the arm and remove the cap. Trim the inside of types as in Figure 137c and e to the same width as the outside piece.

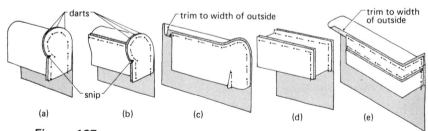

Figure 137

Preparing

Mark the sewing line of darts on the inside with tailor's chalk. Trim and notch the seams as directed on pages 114–15.

Unpin the pieces and use them as a pattern for cutting other caps. Cut other left-arm caps with the wrong side of the 'pattern' to the right side of the piece; cut right-arm caps with the wrong side of the 'pattern' to the wrong side of the piece.

Assemble all the caps, pinning the pieces right-sides-together with notches matching.

Sewing

Make up piping and trim the allowance to ½ in (1.25 cm) as directed on pages 116–18.

Sew darts on the cap bodies as applicable, matching chalk marks. Sew and oversew from edge to point.

Refer to the standard steps for sewing seams of chair/settee covers, for piping and finishing ends of piping with hollow casing and for turning in ends of casing at a hemmed edge. Also refer to the standard steps for pinning, sewing, oversewing and trimming.

Roll arm cap with outside seam (cap over loose cover). Sew piping to the outside piece (Figure 138a). Sew the inside to the outside (Figure 138b). Continue as directed for cap with F/A.

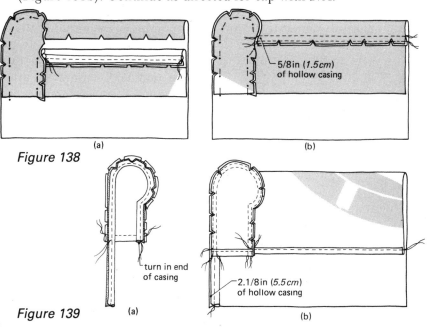

(a)   (b)

5/8 in (*1.5 cm*) of hollow casing

Figure 138

turn in end of casing

2.1/8 in (*5.5 cm*) of hollow casing

Figure 139   (a)   (b)

Cap with F/A.   Sew a double 1 in (2.5 cm) hem at the bottom of the F/A. Sewing piping to the F/A, allowing extra at the inside for piping the inside piece (Figure 139a). Sew a double 1 in (2.5 cm) hem at the bottom of the outside of the body and sew the body to the F/A. Sew extra piping to the inside of the body (Figure 139b).

Cap with T/A.   Sew a double 1 in (2.5 cm) hem at the bottom of the T/A. Sew piping to the inside edge of the T/A, allowing extra for piping the inside piece. Sew piping to the outside (Figure 140a). Sew a double 1 in (2.5 cm) hem at the bottom of the outside piece and sew this piece to the T/A. Sew the inside piece to the T/A, and sew extra piping to the inside piece (Figure 140b).

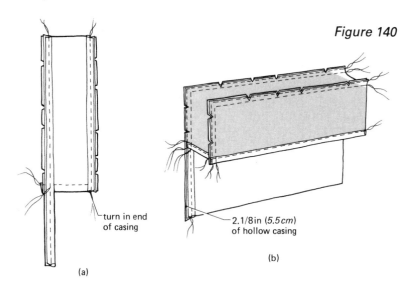

Figure 140

turn in end of casing

2.1/8 in (5.5 cm) of hollow casing

(b)

(a)

Cap with border.   Sew piping to the bottom of the border (Figure 141a), then sew the outside piece to the border (Figure 141b). Continue as directed for a two-piece cap.

Two-piece cap.   Sew piping to the inside piece from the back to the bottom (Figure 142a). Sew a double 1 in (2.5 cm) hem at the bottom of the outside piece and sew this to the inside piece (Figure 142b).

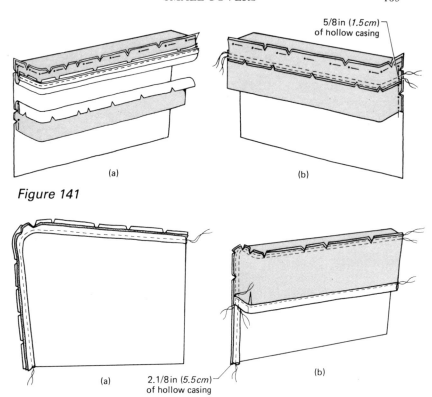

Figure 141

Figure 142

All caps

Stitch seam binding to the allowances at the piped edge of the
inside piece. Slip-stitch the binding to the cover (Figure 143).

Sew a double 1 in (2.5 cm) hem at the bottom of the inside
piece. Sew a double 1 in (2.5 cm) hem at the back of the arm cap.

POUFFE OR STOOL COVER

The following directions are for a round or square pouffe cover
with a gathered skirt (pleats are not suitable); also a round or
square stool cover, with the choice of a gathered or box-pleated
skirt. This kind of cover is easy to make and particularly suitable
for a round pouffe, since it retains its comfortable, dumpy look.

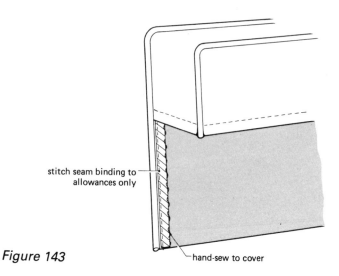

stitch seam binding to
allowances only

Figure 143   hand-sew to cover

Estimating

Seat.   Measure the diameter of a round seat (Figure 144); the length of a square seat (Figure 145). Estimate this measurement plus 1¼ in (3 cm) for seams.

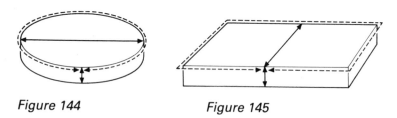

Figure 144   *Figure 145*

Skirt.   Measure the all-round width of a stool seat; the pouffe where plumpest.

Multiply the all-round width × 2 and convert to widths by dividing by 48 in (122 cm). Bring to the greatest number of widths.

Example: All-round width 47 in (119 cm) × 2 = 94 in (238 cm) ÷ 48 in (122 cm) = 1 width and 46 in (116 cm). Estimate 2 widths.

Measure the length to the floor and add 7 in (17.5 cm) for a pouffe (⅝ in (1.5 cm) for the seam, 2 in (5 cm) for the slot; the remainder to go underneath the pouffe); 2⅝ in (6.5 cm) for a stool (⅝ in (1.5 cm) for the seam, 2 in (5 cm) for the hem). Multiply this measurement by the number of widths previously estimated.

Example for a stool skirt: Length to floor 16 in + 2⅝ in = 18⅝ in (41 cm + 6.5 cm = 47.5 cm). Estimate 2 widths (as above) × 18⅝ in (47.5 cm) say 38 in (96 cm).

Pattern with a distinct motif. Estimate 9 in (22 cm) for centring the motif on the seat.

Cutting

Round or square seat, plain or all-over pattern. Cut the amount estimated, measure the width plus allowances from one selvedge and cut from it.

Round or square seat in distinct pattern. If the width of the seat plus allowances is more than 24 in (61 cm), centre the motif on the full width by measuring from the centre up, half the length of the seat plus ⅝ in (1.5 cm) for a seam. Trim at this point, then measure and cut the length estimated for the seat (Figure 146a). Trim the piece equally at the sides to the width of the seat plus allowances (Figure 146b).

If the width plus allowances is no more than 24 in (61 cm) centre the motif on the half width in the same manner (Figure 146c). Cut the width into half widths, and trim the half width for the seat equally at the sides to the width of the seat plus allowances.

Shaping a round seat. Pin the piece face down on the pouffe or stool and rub tailor's chalk over the ridge made by the piping in the upholstery. Trim ⅝ in (1.5 cm) outside the chalk line, correcting any defects due to the upholstery being misshapen through wear. If the item does not have piping, shape as shown in Figure 128, measuring and marking half the diameter of the seat plus ⅝ in (1.5 cm).

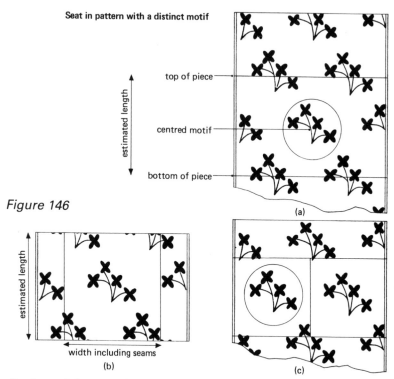

Figure 146

Borders.   Measure the length of the border and add 1¼ in (3 cm) for seams. Cut pieces to this length from the remains of the width estimated for the seat, as follows:

Round seat: Sufficient to make one long border, the circumference of the seat plus 1¼ in (3 cm) for the seam.

Square seat: 2 borders the width of the long side plus seams and 2 borders the width of the short side plus seams.

Piping.   Cut bias strips from the remains of the width for the seat, sufficient to go round the seat and round the bottom of a border. Cut as shown on page 116.

Skirt.   Cut widths as estimated.

Sewing

Make up piping as directed on pages 116–18 and sew to the right side of the seat (Figure 147). Join the ends of the piping as shown on page 139.

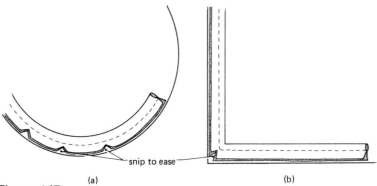

snip to ease

(a) (b)

Figure 147

Border. Join the pieces for a round seat to make one strip, pin it to the seat and sew the join. Pin the pieces for a square seat in place and sew joins at the corners.

Oversew joins in the border and press them open. Sew the border to the seat and oversew with the allowances together (Figure 148). Pipe the bottom of the border (Figure 149).

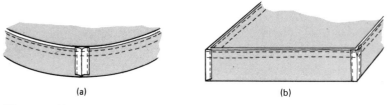

(a) (b)

Figure 148

Figure 149

Gathered skirt. Join the widths to form a flat piece, oversew the joins and press open.

Mark the seat or border at short regular intervals all round; i.e. if the all-round width is 45 in (114 cm) mark every 5 in (12.5 cm). Mark the top of the skirt at intervals twice as long as on the seat. Trim the skirt to the required width plus allowances. Sew the join, oversew and press it open.

Pin the skirt to the seat right-sides-together, matching the marks. Gather between the marks and tack, ensuring that gathers are evenly distributed (Figure 150).

Figure 150

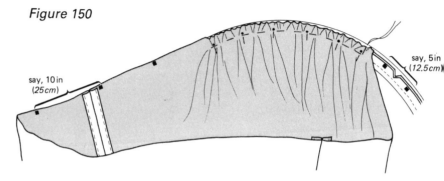

say, 5 in
(12.5 cm)

say, 10 in
(25 cm)

Sew the skirt to the seat (or border) and oversew with the allowances together. Trim to neaten.

Turn up and sew a double 1 in (2.5 cm) hem/slot, leaving a small gap in a slot for inserting a tape.

Pleated skirt.   Join the widths to form a flat piece and oversew the allowances of the joins separately. Pin box pleats as directed on page 136, hiding the joins inside pleats where possible and pressing open those that cannot be hidden. Stay-stitch the pleats ⅜ in (1 cm) from the edge, sewing slowly by machine across the pins. Remove the pins.

Tack the skirt to the seat and trim it to size, allowing for the join. Sew the join and oversew. Sew the skirt to the seat and oversew with the allowances together. Trim to neaten.

Turn up and sew a double 1 in (2.5 cm) hem.

Finishing

Pouffe.   Thread tape through the slot and tie the cover underneath the pouffe. A length of silk cord round the middle of the pouffe is a good finishing touch.

Stool.   Fold 4 × 18 in (46 cm) lengths of tape in half and sew one near each leg, either on the skirt-to-border seam allowance, or the skirt-to-seat seam allowance.

FIXED DINING CHAIR SEATS

Centring and matching a pattern

A pattern with a distinct motif would be expensive for these small covers because the material which is cut out cannot be used elsewhere on the cover. A plain material or an all-over pattern is therefore recommended.

Should you wish to use a distinct pattern however, estimate as explained for the example on page 19, and centre and match the same as for cushion tops/bottoms, page 88.

Estimating

Measure the width and length of the seat where it is widest and longest (Figure 151), and add 4 in (10 cm) for seams to each measurement. Estimate for width and allowances:
Seats up to 24 in (61 cm) wide: 1 width per pair × length of seat
Seats more than 24 in wide: 1 width per seat × length of seat.
Example for 6 seats 23 in (58 cm) wide × 27 in (69 cm) long: 3 widths × 27 in (69 cm) = 81 in (207 cm). Note that for seats up to 27 in (69 cm) wide, 1 width per seat of 31 in (79 cm) wide material would be more suitable.

Figure 151

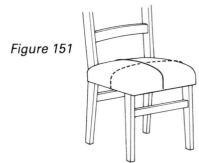

Cutting

Cut the number of widths estimated, each to the required length, then cut the pieces to the width of the seat plus hems.

Fitting

Turn up a double 1 in (2.5 cm) hem at front and sides of the piece and pin it right-side-out on the seat. Pin it with the bottom of the hem level with the upholstery at the front, smooth the piece towards the back and pin it to the chair at the sides. Adjust

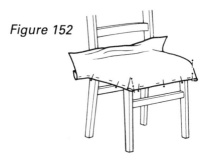

Figure 152

the side hems if necessary and pin darts at the front corners (Figure 152).

The shaping at the back of the seat is not difficult if carried out in stages, cutting away a little material at a time, but it would be a good idea to practise with a spare piece of material on another chair, before tackling the cover.

Pin the cover to the seat around the part to be shaped so that it will not be pulled out of place. Slash at the corners to within about 1 in (2.5 cm) of the upholstery, keeping the slashes straight. (If you slash at an angle you will cut too far). Trim between the slashes (Figure 153a).

Snip almost to the upholstery at the corners. Ease the material round to the back of the seat and trim, allowing about 1 in (2.5 cm) (Figure 153b). Note that the cover should lie quite flat. If it bumps either adjust so that the snips are exactly at the corners or snip a fraction farther.

Take out the pins around the shaping and pin the snipped allowance to the cover to mark the line of shaping (Figure 153c).

Shape and pin the other side in the same way, then pin the back of the seat to the sides. Pin up the material at the back to mark where the hem line should be (Figure 153d).

Part the back-to-side seams and rub tailor's chalk over the pins to mark the openings (Figure 122). Take out the marked pins and remove the cover.

Preparing

Trim the darts to ⅝ in (1.5 cm) and notch through both thicknesses. Trim the back shapings to the fold lines. Trim the back hem allowance to a uniform amount and note the amount for sewing purposes if it is less than 2 in (5 cm). Trim the openings to ½ in (1.25 cm) from the chalk marks (Figure 154).

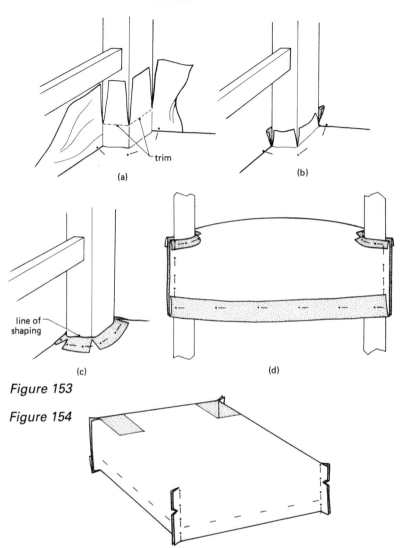

(a)

(b)

line of shaping

(c)

(d)

Figure 153

Figure 154

Undo the hems and darts and use this cover as a pattern for cutting other alike pieces to shape, placing the wrong side of the 'pattern' to the right side of the piece.

Sewing

Sew the darts with notches matching, oversew the allowances and press the darts open. Turn up and sew a double ¾ in (2 cm) hem at the front and sides (so that the cover is a little longer than the upholstery); at the same time, sew into the hems over the front legs two folded lengths of tape each 18 in (46 cm) long (Figure 155).

Figure 155

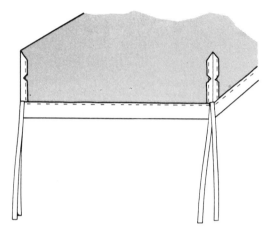

Turn up and sew a ¾ in (2 cm) hem at the back, making it a little longer than the upholstery and turning in whatever allowance is available.

Bind the back shapings with bias strips as shown in Figure 83f, g and h. Bind the openings with 1½ in (4 cm)-wide straight strips as shown in Figure 124, turning in the ends. Sew 9 in (22 cm) lengths of tape into the bottom ends (Figure 156).

Figure 156

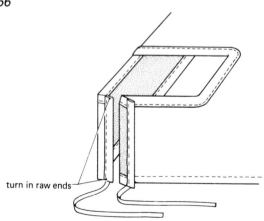

turn in raw ends

Hand-sew hooks to the back edges of the openings and eyes to the side edges.

LIFT-OUT CHAIR SEATS

Centring and matching a pattern
See fixed dining chair seats, page 175.

Estimating
Measure the length of the seat where it is longest (Figure 157) and add 8 in (20 cm). Estimate one width × this amount per pair of seats.

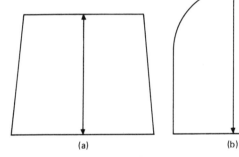

Figure 157

(a)   (b)

Cutting
Cut the number of widths estimated, each to the required length, then cut widths into half widths.

Fitting
Place one half width right-side-out on a seat, centre-to-centre, and pin securely all round. Turn the seat over and pin darts from the corners in. Trim the material between the darts as necessary

Figure 158

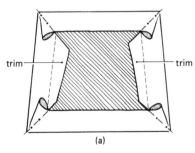

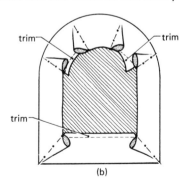

(a)   (b)

to bring the edges even (Figure 158a). If the back of the seat is rounded, shape it with several evenly spaced darts and trim the edges even (Figure 158b).

Trim a dart at the back of the seat to ½ in (1.25 cm) allowance. Part the allowances and rub tailor's chalk over the pins to mark an opening (Figure 122). Take out the marked pins and remove the cover. Note that on a rounded back two darts may have to be opened in order to remove the cover.

Figure 159

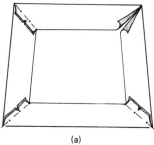
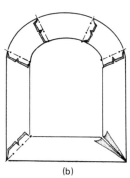

(a)

(b)

Preparing

Trim the remaining darts to ⅝ in (1.5 cm) and notch through both thicknesses (Figure 159).

Unpin the cover and use it as a pattern for cutting other pieces to shape, placing the wrong side of the 'pattern' to the right side of the piece.

Sewing

Sew narrow hems at the edges. Sew darts, matching notches, and oversew with the allowances together (Figure 160).

Figure 160

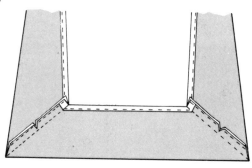

Bind the opening with a 1½ in (4 cm) wide bias strip, turning the ends in (Figure 161). Sew on hooks and eyes.

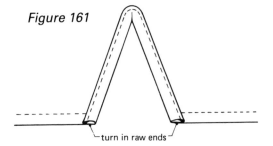

Figure 161

turn in raw ends

INDEX